D1154017

L

Lumumba's Congo: Roots of Conflict

LUMUMBA'S CONGO:
ROOTS OF CONFLICT

by **WASHINGTON OKUMU**
Foreword by Rupert Emerson

IVAN OBOLENSKY, INC.

New York

Copyright © 1963 by Ivan Obolensky, Inc.

Published simultaneously in the Dominion of Canada
by George J. McLeod, Limited, Toronto.

Library of Congress Catalog Card Number: 62-18793
Manufactured in the United States of America
First Printing

THIS BOOK IS DEDICATED

to those sons and daughters of Africa who have perished in the fight for African emancipation, in the hope that they will unite with the living and the unborn in perpetual communion with our ancestors to build a unified and truly independent Africa free from crime and injustice committed against her by colonial exploiters.

Table of Contents

Foreword

This is the book of an angry young man; more significantly, it is the book of an angry young African. Its
subject is the dramatic and tragic series of events which
have marked the history of the Congo since Leopold of
Belgium first undertook to exploit its people and resources,
but in an even more real sense it is the protest of an African against colonialism and against the neo-colonialism
which he sees as menacing the independence which Africa
has won.

The publication of such a book as this is to be hailed
with enthusiasm because it is of vital importance that
Europeans and Americans should be aware of the way in
which Africans look back upon the colonial experience
from which they are now emerging. For the people who
have been on top in the colonial situation it is all too
tempting to forget or to gloss over the fact that the people
who have been the colonial underdogs repudiate colonialism
with passionate bitterness and watch with dread for anything that looks as if it might involve a re-assertion of
white supremacy in whatever guise. The formerly superior
white man has little difficulty in viewing the abuses of
colonialism with great tolerance and concentrating his
attention on the benefits which he believes colonial rule

to have brought. For the African, on the other hand, the key and inescapable abuse from which all the other sins of colonialism flow is the existence of alien rule, establishing the alien as master over the people of the country who are thus automatically deprived of both dignity and equality. As the African sees them the benefits which colonialism is alleged to bring pale into insignificance in the blazing light of this fundamental colonial iniquity.

It is easy for the European and American, now that colonialism has so largely gone into the discard, to assume that the African should overnight forget the colonial experience as he takes his equal place among the nations of the world. That any such expectation is folly seems to me to flow clearly from the testimony of Africans such as the author of this book. The wounds which colonialism inflicted leave psychic scars which will linger long and which any one who has occasion to deal with Africa and Africans must constantly take into account. To tell Africans that they should promptly forgive and forget is of as little immediate consequence as to tell the people of Washington and Moscow that they should forego their animosities and lie down in peace with each other. In examining the affairs of the Congo it is this lesson which Mr. Okumu hammers home. What he has written has the ring of a voice which is authentically African.

On such scores as these I welcome the appearance of this book; but I find it also necessary to suggest that ultimate truth no more rests with Mr. Okumu's side of the argument than with those who have defended the colonial position. There is much in these pages to which I believe Europeans and Americans, even in their capacity as former colonial rulers, are entitled to take objection.

When the author asserts that the task of providing an

objective account of the Congo crisis rests upon "those progressive people who have been able to observe the strife in this great African country intimately, especially the Africans", it is surely in order to protest that the objectivity of such an account is subject to the gravest question. In point of fact, as I have indicated, what I find striking about this book is not its objectivity but precisely the fact that it vigorously reflects what must be the partisanship of most Africans. Thus when Mr. Okumu comments that "there is no doubt at all in anybody's mind that Mobutu, Tshombe, and Kasavubu and their accomplices were the tools of foreign interests in the Congo," the obvious answer is that in the minds of many people—even though they are people whom Mr. Okumu would automatically distrust—there was and continues to be very real doubt. Similarly, much of the attack which Mr. Okumu launches against the attitudes and activities of the United Nations in the Congo would be rejected by many observers whose claim to "objectivity" is as good as his though they set off from different premises.

In the course of his analysis the author returns several times to the theme that independence can be won only by struggle, that the imperialists never give freedom on a silver platter without compulsion. No doubt he and I would continue to disagree even if we were to sit down together to examine recent history in great detail, but I suggest that the record of the postwar years justifies a contrary conclusion at least as well as the one which he has put forward. Particularly in the case of most of the African countries is it difficult to establish that they have won their independence in the last few years as the result of struggles which compelled the imperial powers to relinquish their hold. Indeed, there are sympathetic observers who incline to the view that the lack of a struggle for independence has made more difficult the forging of a sense of national unity in a number of African countries.

It is important that Mr. Okumu's truth should be spread widely on the public record, but it should not be forgotten that there are other truths as well.

RUPERT EMERSON
Professor of Government,
Harvard University

Author's Preface

> For years and years Africa has been the footstool of colonialism and imperialism, exploitation and degradation. From the north to the south, from the east to the west, her sons languished in the chains of slavery and humiliation, and Africa's exploiters and self-appointed controllers of her destiny strode across our land with incredible inhumanity, without mercy, without shame, and without honour. Those days are gone and gone forever, and now I, an African, stand before this august assembly of the United Nations and speak with a voice of peace and freedom, proclaiming to the world the dawn of a new era.
>
> OSAGYEFO DR. KWAME NKRUMAH
> *President of the Republic of Ghana*

This book is the outcome of a study I undertook on my own at Harvard University for the two academic years, 1960-1962, as the result of a visit to the Republic of the Congo in the summer of 1960, where the affairs of the country captured my interest. It was written entirely in spare moments between lectures, examinations, and term papers and during vacations. Although I am not by any means a political scientist, my professional training being in political economy, the amazing "revolution of rising expectations" which had set out to assert man's dignity and had resulted in launching the Congo on a political "take-off," swept me, at least academically, into the political maelstrom. Asia had been transformed from dependency to sovereignty, and "the wind of change" in blowing across Africa had also increased in intensity. In fact, it had become a hurricane.

Until the middle of the nineteenth century the territory drained by the Congo River was practically unknown. But when Henry Morton Stanley reached the mouth of the Congo River in 1877, King Leopold II of the Belgians, realizing the immense possibilities of the Congo, took the lead in exploring and exploiting it and by the Berlin Conference of 1884-85 was recognized as the sovereign head of the Congo Free State. The annexation of the state to Belgium was provided for by the treaty of November 28, 1907, which was approved by the Chambers of the Belgian Legislature in August and September and by the King on October 18, 1908, under the Colonial Charter (last amended in 1959), which provided for the government of the Belgian Congo until the country became independent on June 30, 1960.

On my return from the Congo to the United States of America, I met with the same questions wherever I went to give a speech. The confusion on the subject was incredible. In this first volume of the book, (I hope to work on a second volume) I have endeavored to clarify these issues and my views here are as I expressed them to my American audiences in 1960.

II

This book attempts to analyze the Congo crisis and not to give a chronological account of events. Those who wish to know about the daily happenings during the crisis should consult the United Nations reports and publications or other books already available in this field. In the recent past there has been so much interest shown not only in the Congo crisis but also in the rest of Africa that a work of this nature, which outlines in a simple form the important movements and events that have culminated in the present crisis and provides a close-up of the crisis itself, may be of help to the interested public. There is no need to emphasize the growing importance of Africa to the international community, especially after the Second World War. The Africa of today can be understood only if we cast a quick glance around the world and review the interaction of Africa and the rest of the world. The picture which emerges is an interesting one. Today when we look around the world, we find that time and maturity have enhanced the responsibilities of this once "dormant" continent's responsibilities and problems. Africans consider this not as a cause for panic but as the realization of their own increasingly important and difficult role in international affairs. This role they bravely and willingly accept, as examples of their contributions to the Congo operations indicate.

I have tried to record facts as I know them mainly through several months of personal study and experience in the Republic of the Congo. I have kept under very considerable restraint the sense of political grievances which no progressive African can fail to experience in a crisis of this nature. The book is the outcome of a trip I made to the Republic of the Congo immediately after the granting of independence by the Belgian colonial government on June 30, 1960. My chief object is therefore not to enter into controversial discussion with those who have attempted or are attempting to describe the same things from outside observation. I know that there are many

scientific minded readers with liberal views who will welcome a study of this kind by an African. To those who will
not find the African point of view palatable, I can do no
better than re-echo the writings of Jomo Kenyatta, who
wrote:

> I am well aware that I could not do justice to the
> subject without offending those professional friends
> of the African who are persuaded to maintain their
> friendship for eternity as a sacred duty provided only
> that the African will continue to play the part of an
> ignorant savage so they can monopolise the office of
> interpreting his mind and speaking for him. To such
> people an African who writes on the study of his
> nature is encroaching on their preserves. He is a
> rabbit turned poacher. (See *Facing Mount Kenya* by
> Jomo Kenyatta, pp. xviii)

My visit to the Congo included an extensive tour of
Leopoldville, Eastern Province, Kasai Province, and Equa-
teur Province, areas of intense political strife in the Congo.
I also had an opportunity of meeting prominent leaders
from all shades of Congolese political parties and organizations. I also associated freely with the ordinary people
and attended a conference of independent African states
which was held in Leopoldville during the latter part of
August, 1960. The same trip also took me to the other
parts of Africa including the former Federation of Mali,
Liberia, Ghana, the Union of South Africa (where I was
arrested), the Federation of Rhodesia and Nyasaland,
Kenya and the United Arab Republic, where I have an opportunity to meet prominent African leaders and discuss
African problems, including the Congo situation, with
them. This personal background is mentioned merely
to indicate my deep interest and involvement, though in a

small way, in the political, economic, and social evolution of Africa and my attempt to understand the patterns, the dynamic elements and realities of the cultural, economic, and political aspects of Africa in the background of conjectural history.

III

I could not have written any book at Harvard in the course of my studies without help and inspiration. This is why I must thank Lawrence Ekpebu, a brilliant Nigerian student at Harvard who later migrated to Princeton University. During the extensive discussions we held in our summer apartment in New York, together with Sylvester Ugoh of the University of Nigeria at Nsukka, Lawrence emerged as a debator with an explosive zest of mind. Mr. Indu Chandaria, a Kenya student at Harvard, gave generously of his time during the Christmas vacation of 1960 to help in doing research at Boston University. Chapter 5, with very few alterations, bears the hallmark of his work. I am also grateful to Professor Herbert Spiro, Dr. Paul Sigmund, senior tutor at Quincy House, Harvard, and Dr. Saardia Weltman, a scholar and tutor during my days at Quincy House, for reading part of the manuscript and making very useful criticisms.

I thank Dr. Martin Kilson, a specialist in African politics and lecturer in government at Harvard, for reading part of the manuscript and giving very useful advice. To a certain extent, in fact, Dr. Kilson was my chief mentor during the last stages of the preparation of the book.

My thanks are also due to the distinguished scholar on the Congo, Professor A.A.J. Van Bilsen. With his wide experience as a professor at the Institut Universitaire des Territoires d'Outre-Mer in Antwerp, and adviser to Mr.

Kasavubu at the Brussels Round Table Conference in 1960 and during his Presidency of the Congo Republic until November, 1960, Professor Van Bilsen made his wealth of information and writings freely available to me. I also gained tremendous insight into the problems of the Congo through a series of seminars at the Center for International Affairs, Harvard University. As a research associate in the Center from the autumn of 1961 until July, 1962, Professor Van Bilsen held several seminars on the Congo from which I gained a great deal. Undeniably, the book could not have seen the light of day without his great help.

To all those whose names I have not mentioned, but who helped me in one way or the other, I offer my sincere thanks. I would like particularly to thank Harvard College and the members of the Scholarship Committee and the Financial Aid Office, who looked after my academic and financial shortcomings. Without the aid of such good men as David Henry, Peter Gunes, and others, I would not have been able to accomplish anything. Also, I could not have found a better place than Harvard for reflective thinking. Leaving the hurly-burly of life in the Congo behind me, and coming to that serene academic atmosphere, I was able to look at the African scene more objectively.

I hope that I have not done damage to any reputation! Only in one case do I have any uneasiness. By a series of accidents the distinguished and devoted late U.N. Secretary General, Dag Hammarskjöld, came into sharp conflict with Lumumba at the beginning of the crisis; the part he then played is bound to appear unsympathetic to the reader in one way or the other. It would be impertinent and beyond my competence to attempt an assessment of the causes and ramifications of the disagreement as a whole; I will only say that to the best of my knowledge Dag was a man of most distinguished gifts, who served the U.N. organization notably and could have rendered still greater service in the cause of world peace had he but lived.

Lastly, I am also very thankful to my publishers. In fact, I sometimes wonder that they didn't get tired of my stylistic embarrassments; in any case, they took pains to correct a few errors scattered around, and for this I am deeply grateful.

W. A. JALANGO OKUMU
Harvard University, 1962

Part One

CHAPTER 1

A Manifesto

SINCE THE SECOND World War, one of the most persistent notions in the minds of many people has been that all the dependent nations in Africa are engaged in a militant and irrepressible campaign against alien rule. In the more sensational journalese, this idea is expressed as "kicking the white man out of Africa." In more sophisticated reports the African nationalist phenomenon is portrayed as the maneuvers of a handful of Western-educated, ambitious, and irresponsible "extremists" who want to replace "white tutelage" with "black nationalism." African nationalism is accordingly seen purely in terms of race—black against white. In the Pan-African demands for total independence, total liberation, and total unity, only a rampant racialism is recognized.

A natural consequence of this sometimes uninformed, sometimes malicious, and always unfortunate interpretation of the ideas underlying Pan-Africanism is the deliberate ignoring of such situations as are not punctuated by the now familiar violent clashes between colonial government and dependent people. The world often loses sight of events in countries like Nigeria or Tanganyika in which independence was achieved by negotiation. Negotiations make fewer headlines than events in those areas where nationalist aspirations have been, or are being, forced to find other less desirable outlets—Algeria, the Federation of Rhodesia and Nyasaland, Kenya, and very soon, the "Republic of South Africa" and the Portuguese territories of Angola and Mozambique. Tanganyika under Mr. Julius Nyerere's leadership provides an illuminating example of a dependent territory where the nationalist approach to independence had taken the form of what might be described as "fencing in" rather than "fencing out" all the inhabitants who opt for a common Tanganyikan citizenship regardless of race, skin pigmentation, or national origin.

The most outstanding example of a country where violence has occurred is the Republic of the Congo (Leopoldville). The Congo received her independence June 30, 1960, from Belgium. Nevertheless, the Congo was still substantially a Belgian territory on July 1, 1960. The army of the Congo, known as the Force Publique, was officered by the Belgians. The Congolese relied on Belgium for their lawyers, doctors, and specialists in almost all fields. The proclamation of independence had done little more than give the Congo a head of state and a prime minister whose names were scarcely known outside the big towns in the country.

But a week later the Belgians were plunged in a headlong fight. They were vilified and humbled. Their collapse was swift and total, and nothing remained but street names in Flemish and French. How did it all happen? Faced with such a staggering debacle, we might be excused for seeking an explanation at once simple and all-embracing. In the chapters that follow, I have proceeded with the following questions constantly in mind: Did the Belgians themselves plan it in order to prove that the Congolese were incapable of managing their own affairs? Or, was it the Communists, as has been alleged very often, who intended to penetrate the African continent? Could it have been the Congolese Prime Minister Patrice Lumumba, seeking revenge against the Belgians, who engineered the mutiny of the Force Publique? The Belgians have found too easy an answer—laying the blame on Lumumba. The latter did the same thing—he blamed the Belgians for perpetrating unprovoked aggression against the Congolese territory. Where does the truth lie?

The Congo crisis can be fully comprehended only by viewing the history of the country in the pre-independence era. The Belgians had been very confident, even smug, about their Congo colony. There was no political freedom for the African, no attempt to teach him to be a doctor, a lawyer, or an administrator, while at the same time he was exposed to humiliating racial segregation, making him a subhuman on his own soil. The Belgians did not realize that they were living in the postwar Africa in which the phrase, "Scramble for Africa," had been replaced by the phrase, "African Independence Race," or "Scram from Africa," as Tom Mboya proclaimed at the All-African Peoples Conference in Accra in December, 1958. Even a year before the Congo received her independence, the Belgians had not realized that the final blow to the old concept of European tutelage had been delivered, with the emergence of Ghana in March, 1957, as an independent and completely sovereign state. Instead they were under the illusion that their Congo could be isolated from the "African Independence Race." They were grossly mistaken. The Congolese nationalists had realized that the only solution to the colonial problem lay in political emancipation for their people. "For it is," writes Dr. Kwame Nkrumah, "only when a people are politically free that other races can give them the respect that is due to them. It is impossible to talk of equality of races in any other terms. No people without a government of their own can expect to be treated on the same level as people of independent sovereign states. It is far better to be free to govern or misgovern yourself than to be governed by anybody else."

CHAPTER 2

Leopold's Congo, 1885-1908

To UNDERSTAND the present Congo crisis we must begin with the tragic rule of King Leopold II, the venerable King of the Belgians. Until 1885 most of Africa, then called the Dark Continent, was ruled by native kings and chiefs. But after 1885, the great Western pioneers intervened and began dividing the continent among themselves. Africa then became a mere pawn in European diplomacy. Before this period of colonial expansion, the relationship between Africans and Europeans was different. In earlier centuries, Europeans were not so much concerned with territorial annexations as they were with the procurement of cheap labor for their New World colonies, and as Africa provided a vast reservoir of slaves, the whites bought the blacks and transported them to the Western world.

The raids made upon the west coast of Africa to obtain slaves began in the fifteenth century with the discovery of the West Indies. As Richard Harding Davis points out, it was to spare the natives of these islands, who were unused to and unfitted for manual labor and who in consequence were cruelly treated by the Spaniards, that Las Casas, the Spanish Bishop, first imported slaves from West Africa. Las Casas lived to see the Africans suffer so much more terribly than had the Indians who first obtained his sympathy, that even to his eightieth year he pleaded with the Pope and the king of Spain to undo the wrong he had begun. In the year 1800, William Wilberforce stated in the British House of Commons that British vessels were carrying 38,000 slaves to the West Indies and to the American colonies each year, and when he spoke the traffic had been going on for 250 years. The ship given to one English slave hunter was named by Queen Elizabeth I the *Man of Sorrows*. The diary of an officer on this ship offered the following information: "After going every day on shore to take the inhabitants by burning and despoiling of their towns, our ship was becalmed. But, the Almighty God, who never suffereth his elect to perish, sent us the breeze." As late as 1780, there were advertisements in the United States such as the following example from a Virginia newspaper: "The said fellow is outlawed, and I will give 10 shillings reward for his head severed from his body, or 40 shillings if brought alive." At about the same time, an English captain threw overboard 136 slaves chained together. A jury upheld this maltreatment of human beings, and the Solicitor General said: "What is all this declamation about human beings! This is a case of chattels or goods. It is really so—it is the case of throwing over goods. For the purpose—the purpose of the insurance, they are goods and property; whether right or wrong, we have nothing to do with it." [1]

In 1807, England declared the slave trade illegal. A year later, the United States followed suit, although slavery did not end until the Civil War and the Emancipation Proclamation. European interest in Africa declined after the abolition of the slave trade in 1807. Apart from a few coastal regions in the north and south of the continent settled by white colonists, such as the French in Algeria and the Dutch (Boers) and English in the Cape, Africa was allowed to remain under native tribal rulers. Interest in Africa did not revive until the latter part of the nineteenth century (as George Padmore observes), when economic rivalries among the Western powers gave rise to imperialistic expansion.

This expansion was created by the need for overseas markets, sources of raw materials, national prestige and fresh outlets for the profitable investment of capital. Until these desires arose, colonial annexation was by no means a popular foreign policy in British governing circles. As long as Britain was considered the workshop of the world she had little to fear from foreign competition. But after leading the world for approximately three-quarters of the nineteenth century, English industry was finally challenged by other European powers. Europe was no longer large enough to meet its own needs, and colonies were no longer to be had for the taking. [2]

The Berlin Conference, November, 1884: A conference was convened by the German Chancellor Bismarck in Berlin in November, 1884, at which the powers with colonial ambitions in Africa were invited to negotiate their claims peacefully. [3] After the General Act of the Berlin Conference was signed on February 26, 1885, the three great western European powers—Britain, France and Germany— started in real earnest to annex colonies and protectorates. Britain and France acquired the most territory in Africa, while Germany, a late-comer, got 1,026,229 miles with a population of 16,687,000, covering Togoland and the Cameroons in West Africa, the entire Southwest extending from Portuguese Angola to the Union of South Africa as well as Tanganyika on the east coast. Spain and Portugal were allowed to remain in possession of their ancient colonies. Italy suffered a series of defeats in her attempt to grab Ethiopia in 1887.

The vast and rich colony of the Congo in Central Africa *was granted* to the King of the Belgians, Leopold II, as his personal property. The Congo was taken over by the Belgian government in 1908, following exposures of slavery, forced labor, and other atrocities against the natives. I shall deal with King Leopold's atrocities at some length for they are facts in the history of the Congo and are therefore important to an *objective* analysis of the current crisis which has befallen that unhappy young African nation. These atrocities, which violated the Berlin Treaty, were made public by Sir Roger Casement, the British Consul in the Congo, and the famous English anti-imperialist, E. D. Morel, the great champion and defender of the black race.

The Tragic Rule

The Berlin Conference turned the Congo Basin into an independent state, a "free-for-all" country, where every flag could trade. The General Act of the Conference agreed on the following points:

1. The trade of all nations shall enjoy complete freedom.

2. No power which exercises or shall exercise sovereign rights in the above-mentioned regions shall be allowed *to grant therein a monopoly or favour of any kind in matters of trade.*

3. All the powers exercising sovereign rights or influence in the aforesaid territories bind themselves to watch over the preservation of the native

tribes, and to care for the improvement of *the
condition of their moral and material welfare,
and to help in suppressing slavery.*

These clauses from the Act were binding upon the fourteen powers who participated in the Berlin Conference,
including the United States.

For several years prior to the Conference, King Leopold
had shown considerable interest, as a private individual, in
the Congo. The opening up and development of that territory was apparently his hobby. With his own money he
paid for expeditions into the Congo Basin, employed German and English explorers, and financed protests against
the iniquities of the Arabs, who for ivory and slaves were
raiding the Upper Congo. King Leopold founded the International Association to promote what he called "civilization and trade" in Central Africa, and enlisted the services
of Henry Morton Stanley in this venture. [4]

Leopold's interest in the Congo may have seemed un-
selfish at the time but, knowing him, as we now know him,
as one of the shrewdest of speculators, his self-seeking at
the Berlin Conference may safely be assumed. He presented himself unostentatiously to the members as a candi-
date for the post of administrator of this new territory. On
the surface he seemed an excellent choice: he was the king
of a nation too unimportant to be feared; and of the newly
created state he already possessed an intimate knowledge.
He promised to give his full support to the Dutch, English,
and Portuguese traders, who had been established for many
years in the Congo, and, for those traders still to come, to
maintain the "open door." His professions to help the
natives were profuse. He became the unanimous choice
of the Conference.

We notice next that King Leopold announced to the

fourteen powers participating in the *scramble*-for-Africa Berlin Conference, that he had received from Belgium the right to assume the title of King of the Independent State of the Congo. The powers, without further ado, recognized his title.

Of greatest interest about the King and the Congo was his conception of that country as his own. As one writer put it at the time: "The Congo is owned and the twenty millions of people who inhabit it are owned by one man. The land and its people are his private property. I am not trying to say that he governs the Congo. He does govern it, but that in itself would not be of interest. His claim is that he owns it. Though backed by all the mailed fists in the German Empire, and all the dreadnaughts of the seas, no other modern monarch would make such a claim. It does not sound like anything we have heard since the days and ways of Pharaoh. And the most remarkable feature of it is, that the man who makes this claim is the man who was placed over the Congo as a guardian, to keep it open to the trade of the world, to suppress slavery." And then he continues to show how, in fact, Leopold, while acting under the pretext of suppressing the Arab's raids of the Congo for slaves, substituted a worse form of slavery: "That in the Congo, he has killed slaves and made the products of the land his own, that of the natives he did not kill he has made slaves, is what today gives the Congo its chief interest. It is well to emphasize how this one man stole a march on fourteen powers, including the United States, and stole also an empire of one million square miles." [5]

The remarkable thing, however, about the tyranny of Leopold's private park in the Congo is that no one tried to prevent it. Leopold may have been a man of wonderful ability, in fact he is reputed to have been a wonderful organizer, but we should take notice of the fact that in the fourteen governments that gave him his power, there have been, and there are even today, men if less unscrupulous, of quite as great ability. They are statesmen who are quick to guard the rights of the people they represent. What amazes me is that from the year 1885 to 1908 these statesmen watched King Leopold disobey every provision of the Berlin Conference. Hundreds of thousands of Congolese fled from the Congo, and many of those that remained were mutilated, maimed, or, more mercifully, murdered. And yet the fourteen governments, including the United States, did nothing.

This lack of sympathy for the maltreated Africans is hard to explain. It has been suggested that by 1906, the powers anticipated Belgian control over the Congo. That is, they believed that the Congo would soon be taken over by Belgium, and with Belgium in control, they argued, they would be dealing with a responsible government, instead of with a pirate. Insofar as the Belgium government's take-over was concerned, they were right. But they were not right in their anticipation of an extremely just and responsible government, as I shall show in the following chapter, and it is difficult to believe that the Belgians in the Congo could have been expected to rise above the level of their king so long as Leopold remained King of Belgium. In fact this view led Mr. Richard Harding Davis to say that he would like to see the English take over and administer the Congo. These were his words: "Wherever I visit a colony governed by Englishmen, I find under their administration, in spite of opium in China and gin on the West Coast, that these people are benefited, the Englishman, the native, and the foreign trader from any other part of the world. Of the colonies of what other country can one say the same?"⁶

The first thing King Leopold did in the Congo was to wage war on the Arabs who were raiding the Congo (and Africa in general) for slaves and ivory. He succeeded in driving them out. By these wars he accomplished two things. First, as the defender of the slave, he gained much public credit. Secondly, he kept the ivory. But since war is very expensive, the King soon pointed out to the Berlin Conference that it was unfair to ask him to maintain armies in the field and to administer a great estate out of his own pocket. He therefore humbly sought their permission to levy taxes. It seemed a very reasonable request, because it was going to be difficult to clear the roads, to keep boats upon the great rivers, to mark them with buoys, to maintain wood stations for the steamers, and, finally, to improve the "moral and material welfare of the Natives." These undertakings would cost money, and so Leopold was permitted to levy the few taxes. But it should be noted that after twenty years, none of these improvements could be seen despite the fact that taxes had increased. It was clear that the King did not care about anything in the Congo apart from rubber and ivory. The sole duty of the state and its officers as Leopold saw it was the collection of rubber and ivory. He especially wanted rubber, and he wanted it at once, caring not at all how he obtained it. So he spun the greatest of all "get-rich-quick" schemes— a scheme on a huge scale, full of tragic, hideous, nauseous details.

The only possible way to obtain rubber was through the natives. The white man could not work and live in the teeming forests of the equatorial climate. Earlier, 90 per cent of the Chinese coolies imported there to build a railroad had died.[7] So, with a stroke of the pen, Leopold declared all the rubber in the country the property of the state, and then, to make sure that the natives would work it, ordered that taxes be paid in rubber. "If, once a month (in order to keep the natives steadily at work the taxes were ordered to be paid each month instead of once a year), each village did not bring in so many baskets or rubber the King's cannibal soldiers raided it, *carried off the women as hostages, and made prisoners of the men, or killed and ate them.*"[8]

The King devised a method of paying his agents by results. The more rubber the agent collected the more he personally benefited, and if he obtained it cheaply or for nothing from the natives—by taking hostages, by making prisoners, by the whip of hippopotamus hide, by torture— so much greater his fortune. To dishonesty this method was an invitation and a reward. In my view, it was this system of payment-by-results evolved by Leopold sooner than allow his agents a fixed and sufficient wage, that led to the atrocities. Factual evidence shows that one result of this system was that in seven years the natives condemned to slavery in the rubber forests brought in rubber to the amount of $55,000,000. But its chief results were the destruction of entire villages, the flight from their homes in the Congo of hundreds of thousands of natives, and for those that remained an unthinkable misery. These atrocities were open standard policy. For instance, in the opinion of the state the soldiers, in killing game for food, wasted the state cartridges, and in consequence the soldiers, to show their officers that they did not expend the cartridges extravagantly on antelope and wild boar, produced a human hand (the hand of a man, woman or child) for each empty cartridge. These hands, drying in the sun, could be seen at the ports along the river. Such atrocities continued for well over twenty-five years. One can imagine how many millions of Congolese were killed during Leopold's regime! Every agent in the Congo during that period had to please Leopold (who made no secret of what pleased him). Not only was he responsible for the atrocities, in that he did not try to suppress them, but he was doubly guilty in that he encouraged them. Had he shaken his head they would have ceased. But instead he encouraged these atrocities cynically and callously, without effort at concealment, and without shame. It was even observable that men who, in obtaining rubber through Leopold's tax system, committed unspeakable crimes were rewarded by Leopold with rich bonuses, pensions, higher office, and rapid advancement. Travelers to the Congo pictured the King's behavior in this manner; assuming him to be speaking by himself and saying:

> See how I value that good and faithful servant. That man collected much rubber. You observe I do not ask how he got it. I will not ask you. All you need do is to collect rubber. Use our improved methods. Gum copal rubbed in the kinky hair of the chief and then set on fire burns, so my agents tell me, like vitriol. For collecting rubber the chief is no longer valuable, but to his successor it is an object lesson. Let me recommend also the torture tower, the "hostage" house, and the crucifix. Many other stimulants to labor will no doubt suggest themselves to you and to your cannibal "sentries." Help to make rich and don't fear the state. Go as far as you like.[9]

It is unthinkable that such rule could go on in the Congo without the knowledge of the European powers who signed the Berlin Act. I don't say that there were no

Americans and Englishmen who knew and did not expose
the tragic rule of Leopold. Men like Morel, the American
and English missionaries, the English Consul, Roger Casement, and other men in Belgium fought magnificently
against Leopold; but the Berlin Conference powers to
whom these men appealed decided to be silent, dismissing
such allegations as ridiculous. It was, therefore, only natural that a man of the character of Leopold could take
advantage of this situation. He divided the Congo into
several great territories in which the sole right to work
rubber was conceded to certain persons. Before any
foreigner received permission to collect rubber in the
Congo, he had to submit completely to the King's authority.

One of the most interesting things about Leopold's trade
in the Congo was his claim that through the Congo he
was out of pocket. He said: "this carrying the banner of
civilization in Africa does not pay." Through his press
bureaus he told the world about his sympathy for his black
brother and of his desire to see the commerce of the world
busy along the Congo. These considerations alone it seems
prevented him from giving up what was for him a losing
business. The actual figures of trade in the Congo in 1906
indicate that this claim was a complete lie, and yet it managed to hoodwink the world. One author has written:
". . . in the Kasai Company alone Leopold owns 2,010
shares of stock. Worth originally $50.00 a share, the value
of each share rose to $3,100, making at one time his total
shares worth $5,421,000. In the A.B.I.R. Concession he
owns 1,000 shares, originally worth $100 each, later worth
$940. In the 'vintage years' of 1900 each of these shares
was worth $5,050 and the 1,000 shares thus rose to the
value of $5,050,000." [10]

We should note that only two companies are mentioned

here. Actually there were several companies in which over half the shares were owned by the King. Though he would not reveal the exact figures, a good example was found in the "State Bulletin" publication. The bulletin indicated that the money received in eight years for rubber and ivory gathered in the *Domaine Prive* differed from the amount given for it in the market at Antwerp. The official estimate showed a loss to the government, whereas the actual sales showed that the government, over and above its own estimate of its expenses, instead of losing, made from the *Domaine Prive* alone $10,000,000. We are left to wonder who received that unaccounted-for $10 million!

Certainly the King would not have taken it, for, to cover his generosity in the Congo, he had already reserved for himself another territory known as the Domaine de la Couronne. For years he denied that this existed. He knew nothing of Crown Lands. But finally it was publicly charged in the Belgian Chamber that for years from this private source, which he had said did not exist, Leopold had been drawing an income of $15,000,000. Since then the truth of this statment has been denied, but in the Chamber it was not contradicted.

After this disclosure, King Leopold was faced with terrible "apathy" from the powers who signed the Berlin Conference Act of 1885. He then began to disguise himself as a company, and as a laborer worthy of his hire. He decreed that as a "sovereign" over the Congo, all of the Congo belonged to him. It was as much his property as a staked-out mining claim, as your hat is your property. And the twenty million people who inhabited the Congo during that time were there only on his sufferance.[11] They were his "tenants." He permitted each the hut in which he lived, and the garden adjoining that hut, but his work

must be for Leopold. The natives were not only pro-
hibited from selling ivory or rubber to independent traders,
but if it was found in their possession it was seized; and if
any ordinary person bought a tusk of ivory in the Congo,
the ivory would be taken from them and they could also
be prosecuted. This was the law. Leopold had no respect
for anything else. At Matadi one could see his Prisoners
of the State, each wearing around his neck a steel ring
from which a chain stretched out to the ring of another
prisoner, carrying cargo to the open street. These horrible
atrocities compelled the Powers to send a Commission of
Inquiry in 1904 to the Congo to investigate the atrocities.
The report which was published after four months' work
and an extensive tour of the Congo was shocking. The
charges which were brought against Leopold II as King
of the Congo, were three:

(a) That he had made slaves of the twenty mil-
     lion blacks he promised to protect from the
     Arabs.

(b) That, in spite of his promise to keep the
     Congo open to trade, he had closed it to all
     nations.

(c) That the revenues of the country and all of
     its trade he had retained for himself.

The Commission observed that anyone who visited the
Congo during that time and remained only two weeks
would be convinced that Leopold was guilty of the
charges. In that short time, probably he would not see the
atrocities, but he would see that the natives were slaves,
that no foreigner could trade with them, that in the interest of Leopold alone the country was *milked*. He would
see that the government of Leopold was not a government.

It preserved the prerequisites and outward signs of government. It coined money, issued stamps, collected taxes. But it assumed none of the responsibilities of government. The Congo Free State was only a great trading house. And in it Leopold was the only wholesale and retail trader. He gave a bar of soap for rubber and made a "turnover" of a cup of salt for ivory. He was not a monarch. He was a shopkeeper. As one traveler put it: "And were the country not so rich in rubber and ivory, were the natives not sweated so severely, he also would be a bankrupt shopkeeper. For the Congo is not only a vast trading post, but also it is a trading post badly managed. Even in the republics of Central America where the government changes so frequently, and where each new president is trying to make hay while he can, there is better administration, more done for the people, and the rights of other nations are better respected." (See E.R. Morel's book, *Red Rubber*.)

There is no doubt in my mind whatsoever that, if the Congo were to be properly managed, it would be one of the richest territories on the surface of the earth. But through ignorance and cupidity, it has been despoiled, and is still being despoiled, thereby making its people the most wretched of human beings. Many travelers to the Congo in the early part of this century told tragic stories of how the enslavement of the people continued, and how "they [the conscripts, as they were called] were hunted in the forests by soldiers and brought in chained by the neck like criminals." On hearing these stories one would say that the difference between slavery under Leopold and the slavery under the Arab raiders was that the latter was the better and kinder master. The Arabs did not destroy villages of the natives, nor did they carry off all the black man's livestock, and uproot his vegetable gardens, as Leopold was known to have done. This system was so oppressive that the alleged maltreatment of Belgian nationals by the Congolese after independence in 1960 is nothing in comparison. Any scholar interested in further research on these atrocities can find more than enough material in good universities and other libraries. The Congo was faced with unspeakable atrocities, and the Africans were undoubtedly killed by the millions. Who knows whether the number killed by King Leopold II during his regime surpassed the number of Jews slaughtered by Hitler, Himmler and Co. during the Nazi mania in Germany. This is a work still to be done by African scholars, to expose to the rest of the world how their continent has been the source of great wealth to the other nations through shocking behavior of the Colonial Powers. Anybody with a sense of humanity would hate to grow rich at that price. A quotation from R. H. Davis, one of the travelers in the Congo during the early part of 1905, would be illustrative of the things I have tried to advance in this chapter. He said:

> The dogs in the Kennels of my farm are better housed, better fed, and much better cared for, whether ill or well, than are the twenty millions of blacks along the Congo River. And that these human beings are so ill-treated is due absolutely to the cupidity of one man, and to the apathy of the rest of the world.

NOTES: *Chapter 2*

1. Richard Harding Davis, F.R.G.S., *The Congo and Coasts of Africa* (London: T. Fisher Urwin, 1908) pp. 15-18
2. *Ibid*. pp. 76-78. See also P. T. Moon, *Imperialism and World Politics*, p. 25 (Macmillan)
3. I should like to refer the reader to a book by Henry M. Stanley: *The Congo and the Founding of its Free State*, a story of work and exploration, especially Chapter XXXVIII on the Berlin Con-

ference, pp. 378-458: (London: Sampson Low, Marston, Searle & Rivington, 188 Fleet St., 1885). The reader may also refer to Sir Harry Johnston's *George Grenfell and the Congo* (London: Hutchinson & Co., 1908), pp. 382-496.

4. The author saw in Leopoldville the monument in Stanley Park, which was erected not for Stanley, but to King Leopold himself. This monument became many symbols of colonialism to the Congolese and they decided to damage it. It survives, however.

5. R.H. Davis, *op. cit.*, p. 32.

6. *Ibid*, p. 39.

7. An interesting story goes on in the Congo that Mr. Kasavubu is the child of one of these Chinese laborers imported into the Congo, who as a result of racial miscegenation, have produced many such children in the Congo.

8. R.H. Davis, *op. cit.*, p. 42.

9. It has been said that the degradations and tortures practiced by the men "working on commission" for Leopold are unprintable, but they have been printed, and those who wish to read a calmly compiled, careful, and correct record of their deeds will find it in Mr. E.R. Morel's book, *Red Rubber*. An even better book by the same author on the whole history of the State is his *King Leopold's Rule in the Congo*.

10. R.H. Davis, *op. cit.*, p. 51

11. The present population of the Republic of the Congo is about 14 million. The readers can now imagine what happened to more than six million Africans in the Congo, considering the fact that Leopold ceased ruling the Congo in 1908. Instead of population growing to a peak in 1960, it is still less by six million than the 1885 population. Of course, other factors such as tribal wars, famine, and child mortality would have reduced the population, but not to such an extent! If one can dispute my scepticism, then I would ask him why other parts of Africa with similar circumstances have not suffered from such a rapid decline in population? Leopold's slaughter cannot be exactly determined by anybody because of lack of statistics taken during 1884 to 1908.

CHAPTER 3

Americans in the Congo, 1906

THE ATROCITIES perpetrated by Leopold during his regime failed to move the Berlin Conference powers to humanitarian action. Even after this failure, it is strange that the American traders and businessmen in the Congo never raised protest against Leopold's cold-blooded policies. To understand this, let us examine the history of Americans in the Congo.

In November of 1906, Leopold gave the International Forestry and Mining Company of the Congo mining rights in territories adjoining his private park, the Domaine de la Couronne, and to the American Congo Company he granted the right to work rubber along the Congo River to where it joins the Kasai. This latter is a territory of about four thousand square miles. The American Congo Company had also the option of buying land in any part of a district which was nearly one half of the entire Congo, within the eleven succeeding years, that is, by 1917. Of the Forestry and Mining Company one half of the profits went to Leopold, one fourth to Belgians, and the remaining fourth to the Americans. Of the profits of the American Congo Company, Leopold was entitled to one half and the Americans to the other half.

The American Congo Company originally organized to

exploit a new method of manufacturing crude rubber at the plant. The company was taken over by Thomas F. Ryan and his associates. Back of both of the above companies were the Guggenheims, who were to perform the actual work of running the mines and the rubber plantation. John Hays Hammond, the chief engineer of the Guggenheim Exploration companies, and A. Chester Beatty selected a large number of miners and engineers early in March, 1907, and were sent to explore the territory granted in the mining concession. The legal representative of the syndicates had stated that in the Congo they intended to move "on commercial lines." By that it could be taken to mean that they intended to give the natives a proper price for their labor; and instead of offering "bonuses" and "commissions" to their white employees they would pay them living wages. Many people believed that the American invasion of the Congo would promise good things to that unhappy country under Leopold. Their work to help the Africans would be supplemented by James A. Smith, the British Consul General stationed at Borna, who was considered to be a most intelligent, honest, and fearless young man. The British and Americans were well known during this period as citizens from nations upright in affairs, nations with their full share of philanthropists and humanitarians. And like other rich nations of the West, America and Britain had given large amounts of money to charitable causes to assist those less developed and less fortunate than themselves. These hopes were enhanced by what Mr. Daniel Guggenheim asked Mr. Richard Harding Davis: "Why should you suppose that in the Congo we will treat Negroes harshly? In Mexico we found the natives ill-paid and ill-fed. We fed them and paid them well. Not from any humanitarian ideas, but because it was good business. *It was not good business to cut off a workman's hands or head.* We are not ashamed of the way we have always treated our workmen, and in the Congo we are not going to spoil our record."

Mr. Guggenheim must have said this without realizing that in Mexico he did not have as his partner Leopold, who would tempt him with slave labor, and also that the distance from Broadway to his concessions in the Congo was so great that he could not possibly know in detail what was going on. Of course it can be argued that neither Leopold nor anyone could dictate how the Guggenheim Company was to treat native labor, and that if the company's agents decided to be cruel to the Africans they would be instantly dismissed, but such an argument does not touch the reality of the situation. In any case, nobody can question the sincerity of the American Congo Company, especially in view of their explicit statement accepting full responsibility for what occurred to the natives occupying those areas within their jurisdiction. The only thing which casts some shadow in the minds of humanitarians is the fact that there were men listed for service in the Congo Company who were sure to follow the practices of Leopold himself. They were men who had supported and defended Leopold's dirty work, although they might have done this inadvertently. Mr. Guggenheim, however, seems to have fully intended to give the Africans in the Congo fair treatment, but the fact that he was sitting in New York, which was removed from the scene of operations some four to six months in time and in actual distance approximately eight thousand miles, made it extremely difficult to control the acts of his agents and his partners. He was essentially attacking a problem much more momentous than the handling of Mexican peons or Chinese coolies. In fact, there was a likelihood of these Americans developing the typical European stereotypes (for instance, that Africans were children), and exhibiting symptoms of racial arrogance.

It has been argued that it is very difficult to justify the apparent liberal attitude of Mr. Guggenheim since the Americans went as far out of their way as the Belgians to make a partner of the man who had wrung money from wretched slaves. And, furthermore, the Congo consession could not make the Americans rich, but could only make them richer, as they were already enjoying a high standard of living—it could only mean a figure in ink on a page of a bank book, but what terrible misery it would mean to the slaves.

This argument completely forgets Lenin's theory of imperialism. Imperialism, according to Lenin, may be defined as a stage in the development of world economy in which several advanced capitalist countries stand on a competitive footing with respect to the world market for industrial products; where monopoly capital is the dominant form of capital; and where the contradictions of the accumulative process have reached such maturity that capital export is an outstanding feature of world economic relations. As a consequence of these basic economic conditions, we have two further characteristics: first, severe rivalry in the world market leading alternately to cutthroat competition and international monopoly combines; and secondly, completion of the territorial division of the world by the great capitalist powers.[2]

Imperialism, therefore, comes about when genuine nationalism has been debased. John Stuart Mill described the concept of a nation thus:

A portion of mankind may be said to constitute a nation if they are united among themselves by common sympathies which do not exist between them and others. This feeling of nationality may have been generated by various causes. Sometimes it is the effect of identity of race and descent. Community of language and community of religion greatly contribute to it. But the strongest of all is identity of political antecedents, the possession of a national history and consequent community of recollections, collective pride and humiliation, pleasure and regret, connected with the same incidents in the past.[3]

According to Mill's lucid statement of the limits of nationality quoted above, it becomes quite clear that any attempt to debase this type of genuine nationalism by overreaching its natural boundaries and absorbing the near or distant territory of reluctant and unassimilable peoples results in colonialism on the one hand and imperialism on the other. Colonialism can be described as "the migration of a part of a nation to vacant or sparsely peopled foreign lands, the emigrants carrying with them full rights of citizenship in the mother country, or else establishing local self-government in close conformity with her institutions and under her final control." [4]

Considering these views of colonialism and imperialism, it is easy to see why men who were already as rich as the Americans would have elected to go into partnership with Leopold—the King who got his wealth as a result of unspeakable brutality and acts of genocide. It would have been a wonderful thing, a very fine thing, if these same men, working together, had decided to set free those twenty million people—if, instead of joining hands with

Leopold, they would have overthrown him and freed the Congo. It is my belief that despite the international complications, and considering America's voice at the Berlin Conference in 1885, the Americans could have done it from Washington without much trouble. Only a few lobbies were needed to save the Congo from the atrocities, and in a day Leopold would have been the jest of Europe. But as we know, this was not to be the case. Even today some Americans continue to support Belgian aggression in the Congo,[5] despite the fact that they stoutly oppose colonial suppression by words alone.

As to the questions which would be asked about the outcome of the American advance in the Congo—whether it proved to be the salvation of the Congo, or whether it was a greater evil—I cannot do better than quote the writings of Mr. E. R. Morel, who was the leader in England of the movement for the improvement of the Congo. He wrote:

> It is a little difficult to imagine that the trust magnates are moulded upon the unique model of Leopold II, and are prepared for the asking to become associates in slave-raiding. The trouble is that they probably know nothing about African conditions, that they have been primed by the King with his detestable theories, and are starting their enterprises on the basis that the natives of Central Africa must be regarded as mere "laborers" for the white man's benefit, possessing no right in land nor in the produce of the soil. If Mr. Ryan and his colleagues are going to acquire their rubber over 4,000 square miles, by "commercial methods," we welcome their advent. But we would point out to them that, in such a case, they had better at once abandon all idea of three or four hundred per cent dividends with which the wily

autocrat of Brussels has doubtless primed them. No
such monstrous profits are to be acquired in tropical
Africa under a trade system. If, on the other hand,
the methods they are prepared to adopt are the
methods King Leopold and his other concessionaires
have adopted for the past thirteen years, devasta-
tion and destruction and the raising of more large
bodies of soliders, are their essential accompaniments;
and the widening of the area of the Congo hell is
assured.[6]

This quotation demands no further amplification. Mr.
Morel was right because the charter under which the
American Congo Company had to act was to be granted
by a foreign power, so that whatever they were to do in
the Congo their own government, that is, the American
government, could not hold them responsible. They were
answerable only to the power that issued the Charter; and
that power was "the just, the humane, and the merciful
Leopold." What was going to happen could have been
easily foreseen. But the foreigners who were granted
trading concessions by Leopold did not seem to realize
that his sole idea of administration was to place every black
man in the Congo in slavery. In other words, the only
men the Americans could depend upon for labor were
slaves. The natural question then arises: were the Americans going to use slaves also, or did they intend, as part of
a good business policy, to pay those who would work for
them a living wage? And if they did, at the end of the
fiscal year, having paid a fair price for labor, were they
prepared to accept a smaller profit than would their partner
Leopold, who obtained his labor with the aid of a chain
and a whip? An interview given to the attorney of the
rubber company by a representative of a New York paper

could illustrate further how the Americans undervalued the regime of Leopold. The attorney is reported to have said:

"We have purchased a privilege from a Sovereign State and propose to operate it along purely commercial lines. With King Leopold's management of the Congo affairs in the past, or with what he may do in an administrative way in the future, we have absolutely nothing to do."

When asked: "Under your concessions are you given similar powers over the native blacks as are enjoyed by other concessionaires?" the answer of the attorney as reported, was: "The problem of labor is not mentioned in the concession agreement; neither is the question of local administration. We are left to solve the labor problem in our own way, on a purely commercial basis, and with the question of government we have absolutely nothing whatever to do. The labor problem will not be formidable. Our mills are simple affairs. One man can manage them, and the question of the labor on the rubber concession is reduced to a minimum." [7] This answer by the attorney was a clear manifestation of the ignorance of labor conditions not only in the Congo, but the rest of Africa.

Before embarking on the next Belgian administration in the Congo, it is better to try to understand the motives which led Leopold to allow the Americans to trade in the Congo and the reasons which induced the latter to take his offer. I do not think it is difficult to find the reasons. The Americans wanted the money; they probably did not need it very badly because they were rich already, but they merely wanted it for it would make them richer. On the other hand, Leopold expected to gain in many ways by granting trading concessions to Americans. He definitely wanted more than the half of profits he was to obtain from the Americans, but there was some indication that the Berlin Conference powers were likely to wake up from their apathy and try to cast him out of the Congo. Should this happen, he thought that he could secure the help and support of the United States of America through his American partners. He, therefore, looked to these Americans to kill any action against him that might be taken in the American Senate and House of Representatives, or in the State Department or even in the White House itself. One could probably explain the present behavior of the Belgians in the Congo, especially in Katanga, in similar terms.

NOTES: *Chapter 3*

1. R. H. Davis, *The Congo and Coasts of Africa*, pp. 115-116.
2. Paul M. Sweezy, *The Theory of Capitalist Development* (New York, Monthly Review Press, 1956), p. 307. See also the works of Lenin on imperialism. (Read the entire work.)
3. J. S. Mill, *Representative Government*, Chapter XVI.
4. J. A. Hobson, *Imperialism, A Study* (London, George Allen and Unwin Ltd., 1954), p. 6.
5. When the United Nations was engaged in a military fight to bring Katanga back to the Central Government's jurisdiction, a small section of the American people formed a committee in New York aimed at helping and supporting Katanga's secession financially, politically, and otherwise. Among the prominent members of Congress whose names were mentioned to be connected in one way or other were Senators Dodd from Connecticut and M. Dirksen from Illinois. The latter denied his connection with such a group.
6. Quoted in R. H. Davis, *op. cit.*, pp. 113-114.
7. *Op. cit.*, pp. 105-106.

CHAPTER **4**

Belgian Platonism and Paternalism, 1908-1958

AT LEAST THREE DECADES of benevolent paternalism followed the Belgian government's taking over of the Congo
Independent State from King Leopold II in 1908. The
Congo Free State, due to the efforts of Leopold II and
Henry Morton Stanley, was created in 1885. Its transformation, therefore, into a Belgian colony in 1908 meant
also the doing away of administrative policies current
during the rule of Leopold. Otherwise, the Belgians would
have been faced with a world opinion which had grown
more and more hostile to Leopold's brutality. Also, the
Belgians desired to isolate the Congo completely from the
rest of Africa, and this isolation was to be assured success
by consistent and careful pursuit of paternalistic tendencies.
The Belgian colonial policy indeed might be likened to
Plato's idea of the philosopher-king whose function in
society was to rule while the rest followed. This specializa-
tion of function in society depends upon two factors,
natural aptitude and training. The former is innate while
the latter is a matter of experience and education. The
philosopher-king must therefore be a thoroughly educated
man. Only after long years of training would he be
fitted to run the state.

The only difference with the Belgian policy was that not every colonial ruler was educated. This made no difference to them. Educated or not they all considered themselves to be Plato's philosopher-kings, though it should be noted that Plato talked only of a "Philsopher-King", not of "Philosopher-Kings." They never adhered to the principle of getting the best human capacity and developing it by the best education available. Instead they embarked on a policy wasteful of some of the best brains. The Congo was permanently divided into two groups, Africans and Europeans. European authority and African subordination to this authority were matters of fact. The absolute division between the two worlds was taken for granted. Writing on some current problems of native policy in the Congo in 1954, G. Malengreau says: "Except for certain fundamental liberties, borrowed from the Belgian Constitution, natives and non-whites are under juridicial regimes completely distinct from each other; they are not under the same civil or penal laws, the same social and economic laws, or the same administrative regulations." [1]

In any colonial system where there is legal division between Europeans and Africans, it is apt to be reflected in separate educational institutions and the social services, in the separation of European and African towns, and in a variety of barriers in the way of social intercourse. There was a legal provision in the Congo dating back to 1895 by which it was theoretically possible for the so-called "civilized" Africans to become immatricules and thus enjoy the same civil rights as the Europeans, but this was of little actual consequence. In practice the only method by which an African could escape from his socially subordinate status, and achieve a measure of equality with Europeans, was through the priesthood. This explains why the missions—above all the Catholic missions—had such a formative influence upon Belgian colonial policy. One need only refer to the government statistics on the number of people converted by 1954; out of the total population of about 13,000,000 Africans, roughly 3,455,084 were already Catholics and 704,254 were Protestants. There were in that year well over 25,000 Catholic and 1,357 Protestant missionaries—in all about 7 percent of the total European population (including children).

For obvious reasons, both the Catholic and Protestant missions took a very active part in African education. It became, in fact, a complete monopoly of the missions. This policy of using the missions as the chosen instruments of African education has been traditionally justified partly on the ground of cheapness; but primarily because, it has been argued, only in this way could education be given a positive moral purpose.[2] Thus many Congolese children attended mission schools, and by 1954 there were 743,841 children in grant-aided mission schools. As Thomas Hodgkin summarized:

> ...it is not only when measured in these spectacular, but possibly inflated, quantitative terms that the missions represent a powerful force. Through their teaching and preaching, their rituals and ceremonials, their pastoral and social work, their network of satellite associations, their range of vernacular periodicals and journals, they exercise or seek to exercise, a large measure of control over African minds.[3]

Another very influential group in the Congo is formed by the big Belgian companies with concessionary systems. These great concerns, in the same way that religious institutions wield great spiritual power, have great economic power. The Union Minière du Haut Katanga, Forminere, Huileries du Congo Belge, are the main concessionaries. Their systems play an integral part in the life of the country and, in fact, they account for a much larger proletariat in the Congo than do such systems in most other parts of colonial Africa. It is estimated that in 1953 approximately 25 percent of the population was located outside the native areas and in the "extra-customary" centers of population. This figure represents roughly 37 percent of the tax-payers. Under these circumstances, and due to the fact that these companies contributed substantially to the national revenue, it was to be expected that they would play a large part in the shaping of general policy. The companies greatly accounted, therefore, for the development of the policy of paternalism. Malengreau writes that paternalism meant that workers obtained from the companies lodging, food, clothing, education, medical care, and even amusements. Nothing was left to their own initiative, and they thus suffered from this benevolent guardianship which took from them the very feeling of liberty itself.

It is a commonplace that any officially recognized principle on which a traditional colonial policy is based must have its origin. Thomas Hodgkin provides a clear three-fold origin of policy insofar as Belgium was concerned.

The Catholic conception of society as a hierarchy in which the ruling element is responsible for providing the conditions for a good life for the ruled;

The large corporation's idea of workers' welfare as a means to good industrial relations and maximum output;

And the colonial government's view—that it is desirable and politic to concentrate upon the effort to increase the material prosperity of the mass, and to equip them through education, to play a useful, if subordinate, part, in a modern society, before any moves are made to train an African elite or grant political rights.[4]

Commenting on the effect of paternalism, Hodgkin continues:

Hitherto paternalism has acted as a unifying principle, in relation to which state, church and business have been able to harmonize their sometimes divergent interests. One practical consequence has been that Congolese have on the whole been able to enjoy a higher standard of social services—through an efficiently organized network of hospitals and clinics, foyers, community centers, housing agencies, labour inspectorates, etc.—than exists elsewhere in colonial Africa. At the same time their lives have probably been subjected to more thorough-going regulation and supervision by Europeans—whether as administrative officers, employers and managers, or missionaries—than any other people in colonial Africa.[5]

II

Colonial policies of the various powers differ significantly, although the effects of colonialism on the people are always the same everywhere. The empirical approach by the British to African colonial problems has been clearly described by an authority in British colonial administration, E. W. Evans. He writes, "British practice doubtless pivots on precedent [empirically derived] rather than on principles. But both precedents and principles lead their addicts to much the same destination in the long run; and, as often as not, in the short run. Precedents end in systems. They are only principles in reverse." [6]   Although it would be difficult to maintain that the minds of the British colonial officials are a sort of *tabula rasa*, capable only of receiving and recording impressions, there is one element of British behavior which one might be justified in calling empirical—actions, whether political or not, are made piece-meal, in relation to specific situations or as a means of solving specific problems. For example, in the Lancaster House Constitution (which brought the first African majority into Kenya's Parliament), there were provisions which allowed for tremendous flexibility in view of African aspirations and the rapid political development in Kenya. Thus, in 1961 we had the unique situation of a minority party forming a government, when the African majority party refused to co-operate unless the British government agreed to release Jomo Kenyatta unconditionally. At the same time, other provisions for greater political control by the Africans could be written into the constitution without convening a wholesale constitutional conference.

Another very important aspect of British colonial policy is the specific provision very well stated in the Report of the Watson Commission of Enquiry into Disturbances in the Gold Coast, 1948, Colonial No. 231. It said, *inter alia*: "The Constitution and Government of the Country must be so reshaped as to give every African of ability an opportunity to help to govern the country, so as not only to gain political experience but also to experience political power. We are firmly of the opinion that anything less than this will only stimulate national unrest."

The Devonshire Declaration of 1923 with regard to the paramountcy of African interest whenever there was a conflict between Africans and the European settlers in the colonies is illustrative of the sometimes clear-cut and progressive nature of the British empirical approach, despite certain contradictions. Such contradictions occur, for instance, when the Durham formula, i.e., the liberal conception of the devolution of power from Westminster and Whitehall to the local inhabitants of a dependent territory, is not immediately recognized. We have seen situations in which the concession of self-government to nascent African nations is denied on the basis of the "protection" of white domination and "settler" supremacy. We see today in Southern Rhodesia and Northern Rhodesia, and have seen for a long time in Kenya, a failure to follow the same formal process of devolution of power. A directly contrary policy has been followed—one which grants power to non-Africans.

This concession to immigrant minorities (and primarily European settlers) of increasing political authority over the nascent African nations is an anachronism which must go. It constitutes a game of political poker when, in Central Africa, Britain's policy is not based on traditional liberal-democratic theory—the Benthamite conception that, though men do indeed differ in respect not only of ability and property, but also of moral worth, these differences should be regarded as politically irrelevant; since there is no known method of trying to insure that public policy expresses the general interest otherwise than by granting to each individual as nearly as possible equal rights to take part in the processes of election and government. In West Africa, Britain applied the Benthamite tradition very warily, but the antinomy underlying this tradition can be seen in the failure of Britain to tell Sir Roy Welensky (the Prime Minister of the so-called Federation of Rhodesia and Nyasaland) the truth. The behind-the-scenes lobbies of Sir Roy (and people who think like him) during the Review of the Constitutional Conference in London fails to take account of the fact that no plan in Central Africa, be it political, economic, or social, can ever hope to succeed without the express consent, support, and co-operation of the indigenous African people.

The adoption of a parliamentary system is supposed to be the beginning of a *national* system of representation. Parliaments fail if they cater to purely sectional or communal interests, or estates, rather than persons. They have failed in Central Africa to provide Africans with representation commensurate with their numbers in the community, an electoral system through which they can enjoy the experience of choosing their own ruler, and an effective measure of administrative and executive power. It is only natural that under these intolerable conditions, the nationalists must fight unconditionally to transform these legislative bodies from an Estates-General into a popularly elected National Parliament.

In principle Africans in British colonies can organize for political and industrial purposes; they can move freely within their own countries and travel abroad, and they can, generally, engage in nationalist activities which are not tolerated in the Portuguese, Belgian, and Boer rule. Nevertheless, the actual legal and administrative restrictions imposed by British and other colonial governments upon nationalist leaders and organizations through sedition laws, states of emergency, control over migration, police surveillance, etc., are quite contradictory.

III

Looking at the French Cartesian approach, which the French would rather like to compare with British "empiricism," we see a quite different policy. It is worth noting

here that the words Platonism, Empiricism, and Cartesian-
ism are some of those neat generalizations which are only
partially true, although they may have certain practical
purposes. Scholars in this general field have made very
interesting observations on these policies. For example,
Hodgkin says:

> Of course, the French do not really begin with a
> few self-evident axioms about France's relations with
> French Africa, from which they proceed to deduce a
> variety of propositions covering all aspects of policy
> and administration. Nor do the British reject all
> assumptions and live entirely from hand to mouth.
> But the French are certainly more interested in the
> effort to make their system coherent and intelligible;
> and are more conscious of, and worried about, its
> actual illogicalities and its inconsistencies. And, with
> their much more centralizing habits of thought and
> methods of government, they have achieved a measure
> of uniformity in the pattern of institutions which
> they have introduced into *Afrique Noire* that is alto-
> gether lacking in British Africa. Though even in
> this there is, inevitably, a gap between theory and
> practice: political and legal institutions which are
> formally identical do not in fact work out in the
> same way in Senegal, with the liberal-socialist tradi-
> tion, and in Chad, the stronghold of Gaullism.[7]

It has been argued that the French colonial policy cannot be understood in terms of the conventional textbook
distinction between "assimilation" and "association," to
which words much importance has been attached. Mr.
Kenneth E. Robinson, writing on political development in
French West Africa (in Calvin Stillman, *Africa in the
Modern World*, 1955) has suggested two distinguishing
terms to describe French colonial policy, namely "identity"

and "paternalism." These two policies bear some relation to the revolutionary-equalitarian and conservative-autocratic phases in French internal history. Identity seeks in principle to establish in the colonial country institutions identical with those in France. According to this policy, all men domiciled in French colonies, without distinction of color, were French citizens, and enjoyed all the rights assured by the constitution. Institutionally, this principle was given expression in citizen rights—including, after 1948, the right to elect a deputy to the French Assembly.

In spite of all these niceties, the Cartesian approach never fully succeeded. Furthermore, the changing social and political climate in Africa today necessitates a change in administrative attitudes. But even now there are unequivocal signs of postwar, post-independence French policy. Contradictions appear at once when one examines the professions of attitude and what actually happens in practice. In theory, the French civilization is conceived as universal—an open society in which no attention is paid to race or nationality, and men are valued simply in relation to merit and intelligence. This would necessarily mean that a bridge, instead of a wall, is built between the different races. However, in practice, the French who live in Africa have been as liable as any other white men to develop the typical white stereotypes (Africans are still children, etc.). Many still exhibit symptoms of racial arrogance. The constitution of the Fourth Republic embodies the principle that all Africans in the French territories, and as French citizens, were supposed to enjoy equal political rights with metropolitan Frenchmen. Popular participation in the processes of government, with an electoral system near universal adult suffrage, was to be granted. The expansion of opportunities for higher education with a view to building up a growing African elite capable of discharging administrative and specialist functions on equal terms with Frenchmen was greatly stressed. The French also recognized in theory that equality of political rights has limited value unless accompanied by a deliberate effort to abolish gross inequalities of economic standards and opportunities. This implied that the metropolitan country had to spend heavily for the development of the African economies.

All these ideas were, as said, to a large extent good only on paper. The establishment of the system of "dual college," which was operative throughout the French territories, only gave more weight to the votes of the metropolitan Frenchman as compared to the African votes. Although Africans could be elected to represent their people in the French Parliament, the wholly inadequate representation of Africans made a mockery of the whole scheme, considering its population as compared with that of France. The electoral arrangements were such that Africans could never have effective control of, or a substantial share in, executive power. The system provided for representative, but not responsible, government. Hence the administration appeared as a quasi-independent power, much influenced still by the principle of paternalism and very little by elected representatives. This meant that the administrative hierarchy remained dominated by Frenchmen. Little progress, if any, was in fact made with Africanization, either in public or private concerns. It is even known that in many cases career prospects for the university-educated African elite were somehow restricted. And on the economic side the ever-widening gap between the African and the European, which constituted the extreme inequality rampant in many African states, pointed toward a legacy with which many emergent states in Africa have to contend.

IV

How does all this compare with the Belgian Platonic approach? More often than not, the Belgians claim that their colonial policy is "empirical": a statement sometimes accepted as valid, but now being subjected to a process of examination and doubt.[8] The most often heard claim of the Belgian national character is that they are essentially a bourgeois nation—a nation of townspeople—in whose history the self-governing commune has played a very important part. That they are a people "whose paintings reflect the esteem in which the prosperous burgher, the civic dignitary, the comfortable middle-class family circle, have traditionally been held." And that they are a people normally overlaid by "a common belief in what are sometimes regarded as Protestant values—material success, thrift, self-help, domestic decency and comfort, respectability; in the Calvinist gospel of work; and in the small monogamous property-owning family as the pivot of society." [9]

This would imply that for a person to be considered civilized, he must accept and act upon these moral beliefs. Thus, one idea which, in spite of deviations, did profoundly influence Belgian policy was the idea of a civilizing mission to the Congolese people, which in a sense meant training them to be good burghers, organizing their lives and behavior on the basis of Belgian middle-class values.

Nevertheless the one factor which the Belgians completely forgot was the exportation to the Congo of certain vices as well as virtues, in the way that the French have exported theories such as Existentialism and Neo-Thomism,

Gaullism and Communism to their former possession in West Africa. In the case of Belgium, the very intense differences and disagreements between Flamands and Wallons, between Catholics and Anti-Clericals are real enough, and these have been exported to the Congo. But the Platonic nature of Belgium's paternalistic approach has completely eliminated the chance of the Congolese meeting more profound ideas and traditions. Thomas Hodgkin, commenting on the Belgian Platonism, vividly writes:

> Platonism is implicit in the sharp distinction, social and legal, between Belgian philosopher-kings and the mass of African producers; in the conception of education as primarily concerned with the transmission of certain unquestioned and unquestionable moral values, and intimately related to status and function; in the belief that the thought and behavior of the mass is plastic, and can be refashioned by a benevolent, wise and highly trained elite; that the prime interest of the mass is in welfare and consumer goods—football and bicycles—not liberty; and in the conviction that it is possible, by expert administration, to arrest social and political change.[10]

Scientists believe that the only tragedy is to have a hypothesis killed by a fact. In Africa, the facts of political life have killed various tangled messes of hypotheses conceived by European powers to be the basis on which their colonial possessions were to be governed. Africans have reacted accordingly to their subjugation and have condemned the lack of political outlets for their peoples. The Congo provides one of the clearest examples. Belgian emphasis upon economic expansion (involving not only mining and cash-crops but also secondary industries, with the social result of producing a politically minded and prosperous

Congolese middle class, a class of skilled workers, and a swollen unskilled proletariat) was meaningless without creating political outlets for these new classes. The Congolese living in great towns and cities were encouraged not only to think, but also to act, as Economic Men. I have dealt with these problems in more detail in the next chapter. Suffice it to say here that the African reaction to all this was inevitable.

In 1956 a group of politically minded Congolese published, in the July-August issue of a small African paper in Leopoldville, a historic document called the *Conscience Africaine*. This document was a call by the Congolese leaders to fight for complete political emancipation and decolonization of their people, and was composed by a culturally minded group which had emerged in Leopoldville under the leadership of Joseph Malula. In it they seriously discussed the various sociological, philosophical, and psychological problems facing them. Joseph Ileo, who later became Kasavubu's Prime Minister when the first premier, Patrice Lumumba, was assassinated, was among its drafters. The *Conscience Africaine*, which spelled out a complete break with paternalism, is reproduced in full in Appendix B.

The Manifesto of the *Conscience Africaine* completely awakened especially those people who appeared to be drowning ever deeper in a sea of "sin" and, even more, those who had become more and more confused in a sea of fantasy, as many European settlers have been. The sudden revolt against paternalism was the result.

NOTES: *Chapter 4*

1. Malengreau, G. "Some Current Problems of Native Policy in the Belgian Congo." (1954 unpublished)
2. On Belgian Educational Policy, see J. Vanhove, "L'Oeuvre d'Educa-

tion au Congo Belge et au Ruanda Urundi" (Encyclopedia du Congo Belge, 1953)

3. Hodgkin, Thomas. *Nationalism in Colonial Africa* (New York University Press, 1957) p. 50. Also see Congo Belge, Counseil de Gouvernement. Statistiques. 1955
4. Hodgkin, Thomas. *Ibid.*, pp. 51-52
5. *Ibid*, p. 52
6. Evans, E. W. "Principles and Methods of Administration in the British Colonial Empire" (Colston Papers)
7. Thomas Hodgkin, *op. cit.*, pp. 33-34
8. J. J. Maquet: *Modern Evolution of African Populations in the Belgian Congo* (Africa, XIX, 4 Oct. 1949). This is a very useful account of development in Belgian policy up to 1949. For the more recent period, see A. F. G. Marzorati, "The Belgian Congo" (*African Affairs*, LIII, 231, April, 1954) and G. Malengreau, "Recent Developments in Belgian Africa" (in Grove Haines, *Africa Today*)
9. Thomas Hodgkin, *op. cit.*, p. 48
10. Thomas Hodgkin, *Ibid*, p. 52.

CHAPTER 5

The Sudden Revolt
Against Paternalism

THE TITLE OF THIS CHAPTER does not quite describe the recent chain of events in the Congo. The actual revolt against the paternalistic policies of the Belgian government seemed to occur suddenly, in the last three or four years, but it must be emphasized that there has been a growing body of discontent against the policy of paternalism ever since the Second World War. Various factors, with which we will deal later, accounted for this change in outlook. But the main thesis of this analysis is that it was inevitable that the Congolese would oppose violently the paternalistic policies of the Belgium government, since certain basic assumptions at the very foundations of the Belgian policy were unsound. These assumptions were based on Utopian hopes rather than on careful empirical study of the local situation. Nor were the assumptions flexible so that they could fairly easily accommodate any needed change.

Let us consider the assumptions on which the Belgian policy has been based. There are five fundamental principles that the Belgians have hoped would exist at all times in the affairs of the Congo—if not for all time, at least till the perfect theoretical plan of the Belgians was fulfilled. The first principle was: isolation of the Belgian Congo from the rest of the African continent. By doing this, the Belgians believed they could avoid the infiltration of nationalistic ideas and the beginnings of any independence movements in the Congo. They were too naive in this belief of theirs. How could they stop the penetration into the Congo of the ideas current in the whole of colonial Africa? They would have had to build an enormous iron curtain to see that no alien ideas crossed the Congolese border. After all, the Congo is a very big country, surrounded by other nations which have very strong nationalistic movements. With the high speed of modern systems of communication it would be extremely difficult to stop nationally conscious leaders from making a bridge to the rest of Africa; and with the increasing spread of education and literacy it would be impossible to stop students from reading revolutionary works—unless there was a *very* efficient system of censorship and police control.

And, if the Belgians wanted an isolated Congo, they were wrong in emphasizing only the economic progress of the Congolese. But that was the second principle: material progress without social and political improvements. This is perhaps the fundamental fallacy of the whole Belgian paternalistic policy—in an area where the other imperialists did not do as badly as the Belgians, and for which they deserve more credit than the Belgians.

Economic progress of the Congo created a prosperous Congolese middle class of technical elite doing skilled work, and small private businessmen who undertook a variety of ordinary jobs in all fields. The members of this middle class, mainly centered in the urban areas, especially the big towns, were practically trained to think in terms of

Economic Men. They looked at everything from a monetary point of view—they thought in terms of how much more they could buy of goods and services if they worked a few extra hours. They were almost taught that material wealth was an end in itself. However, they were not given an opportunity to involve themselves in political activities. Nor was there much initiative left with which the Africans could organize their own social life. Opportunity and initiative were both the prerogatives of the government and the Church and they were the organs through which social activity was organized. This left not too much room for the free expression of the African's mind. Everything was done for him. He was treated like a child. He was never taught to take the initiative to do something that he desired. Every time, the individual was either told what to do by his guardian, the state or the Church, or the same authorities did the thing for him instead of letting him at least do it by himself. This state of affairs could definitely not exist for very long. The African was becoming impatient. He wanted freedom of expression. He wanted to run his own clubs and organizations. In brief, he wanted to be somebody—a part of a society, and not merely an instrument in the mechanism of national economy.

An even more emotional area is covered by the third principle: actual practice of good race relationships is unimportant. In theory there was supposed to be no color bar in the Congo. The government was supposed to pursue a policy whereby the Europeans and the Africans could work and live harmoniously with each other. But this supposition was not quite fulfilled in practice. There were formal and informal barriers between the whites and the blacks. This was resented the most by the *évolués*, whose problem we will deal with later.

The fourth assumption of the Belgians was that the

domestic politics of Belgium could be kept apart from the Congo. They thought that the party politics of Brussels should not be made evident to the Congolese, for they wanted to present a picture of a united Belgium. Within the Congo, they had hoped that the traditional union of the state, the Church and the companies would continue, so that the government could efficiently carry out her policies: there would be no economic or religious interests to oppose the policies of the government. But this pre-war situation had been shaken after the war. The solid union between the state, the Church and the companies existed no more, and the Congolese could exploit the splits in the Belgian domestic parties.

And, the fifth principle: Belgian theory of colonial government should be used at all times. This assumed, of course, that the Belgian theory was actually good; but, be that as it may, it is clear that the extreme theoretical basis on which the Belgian Congo was ruled from Brussels did not make it any easier to maintain Belgian rule effectively in the Congo for too long a time. All the important orders came from Brussels. The entire administration was too centralized. Often the advice of the persons who had spent most of their lives in the Congo and knew the situation pretty well was not utilized.

Let us consider the above five points in greater detail in the following sections.

I

The Belgian Congo was supposed to be isolated from the rest of the continent and to be insulated from foreign influences. But the Second World War saw the first significant break in this isolationist policy. Congolese troops were sent abroad to fight the enemies of the Allies. For the first time they were exposed to some very new ideas and concepts of which they had not been aware under the Belgian paternalistic policies. Again, it was the first time that a significant number of the Congolese had had a chance to see the world outside their homeland. This had profound effects upon them. The greatest impact of the war was to change the African's view of the European. He was no longer regarded as highly as he had been before the war. The Congolese had seen brutal killings of white men by other white men. The Europeans were not as perfect as they had pretended to be in the Congo. On many occasions the Congolese soldiers, in military uniform, had opportunities to order the Europeans. Many had seen Europeans who lived as poorly as many of the Congolese did. This impact of the war not only changed their attitude toward the Europeans, but it also injected new ideas of improving their conditions in every respect. The war opened the eyes of the Congolese and showed them their potential capabilities to do things which were at that time exclusively limited to the Europeans. They had seen good things in other countries which they were desirous of attaining for themselves. The American Negroes serving in the army were treated as the equals of the whites, and this set a new precedent in the eyes of the Congolese. "Why couldn't we obtain the same treatment as the white man in our country?" they asked. They had also seen the Asians manage their own affairs and be in charge of responsible jobs in all spheres. They were asking, "When will we be able to play a responsible part in the government of our own country?" No revolution occurred overnight, but by the end of the war the seeds of a process of change were sown. The isola-

tionist policy could not last now for too long. The Congo
was no longer insulated against external influences.

An even more important influence than the Congolese
experience in the war was the continuous infiltration of
ideas that helped create the first feelings of nationalism
in the Congo. This infiltration occurred from the rest
of colonial Africa while it was trying to get loose from
the chains of imperialism. The cry of independence had
dominated the colonial people. They were no longer
prepared to be bound to the dominating and totalitarian
minorities that ruled them either from their own countries
or from the metropolitan countries. They were asking
rightfully for the recognition of their demand for freedom. By the end of the war most of the countries in
colonial Africa had the beginnings of the nationalistic
movements which would ultimately attain freedom from
foreign rulers. The importance and the influence of these
movements was growing at an astronomical rate. More
and more people were taking interest in the movement.
Over the week-ends, mass meetings (where allowed by
the colonial government) demanding freedom, superseded
social events. Those who could not read asked those who
could read to tell them what was said in the newspapers.
Most of those people who had access to news were interested in the movement for freedom. Under such circumstances, how could one expect the Congolese to remain aloof from this rising force? The Belgians would
have had to devise a very efficient system to suppress
the desires of the Congolese and insure that no external
influence penetrated the Congo. But to undertake such
a measure she would have had to face an increasing amount
of resentment against imperialism which was growing in
the world and in the United Nations with its increasing

number of Afro-Asian countries who had once been under colonial rule. Belgium could, and did, maintain strong immigration and emigration laws. Until recently, it was very difficult for young ambitious Africans to leave or enter the Congo. And similar restrictions for entry of foreign books and magazines were enforced by the Belgians.

But in spite of the attempt by the Belgians to stop the influence of foreign countries entering the Congo, they could not restrict it absolutely. The nearest center of nationalism was just across the river from Leopoldville— in Brazzaville. One could practically swim from one town to the other! Here, on August 24, 1958, a very significant event occurred: an event that really set the ball of nationalism rolling. General Charles de Gaulle was paying a visit to this city, the capital of the French Congo. His mission was to deliver a very important message to the people of the French Congo. He wanted to tell them, "whoever desires independence can immediately obtain it"! The Congolese couldn't believe it! Hundreds had crossed the river to hear the General's speech. They were amazed to hear that you could have independence for the asking. They didn't expect this to happen in the Belgian Congo for a long time. But one of the more important persons present at this speech was Patrice Lumumba. Mr. Lumumba was quick to realize the significance of this to his own country, and the Mouvement National Congolais (M.N.C.) was started by him at that time.

Influences from the rest of the African countries of course helped to formulate these first feelings of nationalism. The developments in the Copperbelt district of Northern Rhodesia, just across from the wealthy Katanga

Province, definitely had an impact on the Congolese.
Similar influence was exerted by the East African countries. There were a few Congolese working in Uganda
who were exposed to the East African nationalist movements. The eastern parts of the Congo spoke the same
language, Kiswahili, as the East Africans, and this reduced
the problem of language barriers. Radio Cairo also exerted
its influence via the Kiswahili programs. Further, reports
of the situation that existed in the Union of South Africa,
Southern Rhodesia and Kenya were better publicized.
This made some of the forward-looking Africans in the
Congo apprehensive of their own future, and more cautious
of the Belgian policies. Recent positive declarations of independence in the West African countries further stimu-
lated the nationalistic inspirations of the Congolese.

Two more events of very decisive importance occurred
in this area of Congolese relations with the external world.
The first was the Brussels World Fair. At this great world
event a huge area was reserved for the Congo and Ruanda
Urundi. Hundreds of Congolese were taken to Brussels
to do jobs of all kinds in the booths. They were in charge
of the Information Center of the Congo, guarding some
of the exhibits, or just acting as ushers. At the Fair, they
had an opportunity to meet people from all parts of the
world and talk to them. They were asked many questions
which opened new visions in their thinking. They had
the opportunity to see the stands of many peoples and
observe their ways of life, see what their countries did and
looked like, and compare their own condition in the
Congo with that of the foreigners. When they were away
from the Fair, they saw Belgian life, and naturally compared it with the life which the Belgians lived in the
Congo. They found a fantastic difference. The opinions

they formed were not going to be liked by the Belgians in the Congo. Moreover, when they would return home, they would spread about what they had seen to their friends and relatives—and this type of news circulates very rapidly and efficiently in the Congo! By now, Belgian attempts to isolate the Congo were absolutely impossible.

The final event that completely shattered the iron curtain of Belgium around the Congo was the decision of the Belgian Congo's government to let Patrice Lumumba and two other Congolese travel to Accra for the All-African People's Conference. Here, in Accra, extra fuel was added to the already burning nationalism of the Congo. The Congolese at the Conference were impressed by the solidarity of the African independence movement. Resolutions were passed that no African country should be under colonial rule after 1961. Mr. Lumumba supported this with the greatest vigor, and said so in a speech which he made in Leopoldville after his return from Accra. At the Conference itself he said:

> This historic conference which brings us together, politicians of all the countries of Africa, shows us that in spite of the frontiers and the ethnic differences, we are of one mind and have the same desire to make our continent a happy one, free from anxiety, and from the fear of colonial domination. Down with colonialism and tribalism! Long live the Congolese nation. Long live an independent Africa!

Belgium had failed to isolate the Congo successfully.

II

The Belgian policy had favored the creation of a growing middle class, but comparable progress in social and political developments of this class was not permitted. This increasingly prosperous group of Congolese, who came to be known as the évolués by the Belgians, were denied the freedom to express freely their political and social beliefs. There were five main areas in which this deficiency was felt the most: education; free press; free social activities; problems in urban areas; and the suppression of political activities. We will deal with each separately, but before we do that a brief comment on the évolués might be helpful.

An understanding of the évolués is absolutely vital to appreciate the recent history of the Congo and to understand its future actions. Emerging évolués will be responsible for introducing new ideas in the Congo in the future. Their actions will mold the course of development that country is going to take in the future. Their views will decide what form of country the Congo is going to be. In short, they will be the leaders of the Congo.

Most of the évolués are young—few are much older than forty. This definitely has a tendency to make them less conformist and more easily accessible to new ideas. If it is possible to generalize at all, we might even conclude that their youth might make them less cautious as compared to older people. But these are generalizations into which not too much should be read.

Most of the évolués are either educated in the Western way or they are self-made enterprising individuals. They have attained their existing positions through ability rather than by inheritance or social background. They had to move up the ladder from the very first step. They were not given a head start by being placed at the middle or top and they definitely were not carried up in an elevator.

Those that take part in political activities rarely have an

established and secure financial position as is the case in the European countries and in America. Politicians in these older countries of Europe and America have sound and secure family estates on which they can rely if they are unsuccessful or suddenly thrown out of politics. In Africa this is not usually the case. The Africans have to depend on the income they receive from their political activities.

Education

The problem of education is a threefold one: lack of facilities for higher education; monopoly of education by missionaries; and education for women. It is these three aspects of the problem that hindered the social progress of the Congolese, especially that of the évolués. It is in these areas that economic progress was keeping ahead of the social progress of the évolués. Let us consider these points more carefully.

Greatest tribute should be paid to the Belgians for instituting one of the finest and most extensive systems of primary education in the Congo as compared to what most of the other colonial powers have done. But at the same time one cannot but notice the stupidity of the Belgians in assuming that, after he has received a primary education, a student can suddenly be told his education has ended. This might, and in fact does, work for a majority of cases. *But* there is a significant minority for which this is absolutely wrong: the minority who really get involved in their studies and for whom neither formal nor informal education ends for a considerably longer period. They are the intellectuals. By being deprived of their intellectual pursuits they are not only done harm, but the potential

ability that exists in the country is not being utilized. Harm
is done to both the individual and the society. To the ambitious African student, and there are quite a few of them,
being deprived of the chance to study means a great deal.
As one African put it: "In Africa, education is the greatest thing."

Today there are 1,200,000 Congolese children in primary schools, but fewer than 10,000 reach high school.
Vocational schools train another 17,000 students. Hence
one student in every 120 reaches high school, and one in
every 47 has some form of training after leaving primary
school. At college level, there are two institutions in all
to cater to all these students. There is the Catholic University of Lavanium in Leopoldville with 365 students, and
the State University in Elizabethville, with 219 students,
which was started in 1956. Clearly the facilities for higher
education are very inadequate. Moreover, only a few
students were allowed to study abroad. This inadequacy
in higher education is resented very much by the Congolese, especially by the évolués who suffer the most from it.

Not only were the poor facilities for higher education
criticized, but also there was a very strong and increasing
feeling against a religiously dominated educational system.
The Belgian government had given monopoly rights of
education to the religious groups. Most of the schools
were missionary schools. Until 1956 the only university
that existed was a Catholic university. The mission schools
accepted only students who would follow the same religion as the mission. Hence if you lived in an area where
there was only one school, let us say one run by a Catholic
mission, if you were a Protestant or not a Christian, you
would have to change the religion of your child so he

could go to a mission school. This sort of thing is fairly common and is resented by the Africans. What this arrangement in fact means is that if you want to study, your religion will be determined by the mission school that is nearest to you. This is absurd. It is a hindrance to the freedom of thought.

Furthermore, the teaching in the mission schools was based too much on religion. Many students did not like this at all. It restricted the horizon of thought of the student. Many a time the teachings in their schools would be quite contradictory to what they had traditionally been brought up to believe. This confuses a student. He doesn't know what to believe in. Many times he is lost; he has confidence in nothing. It generates a crisis within the individual which is not easy to erase for a long time, or the crisis may even continue for the rest of his life. It gives him a feeling of insecurity. The only escape from this moral crisis is to accept dogmatically what he has been brought up to think either at his school or at his home.

Finally, the Belgians had done very little toward the education of women. A very small proportion of the school-aged girls went to the schools. It would be unfair to accuse the Belgians of not doing enough, but they can be criticized severely for their emphasis on only one aspect of education—primary education for boys. Their educational policy was unbalanced, with too much weight at the male end and too little at the female end.

Education for women is good in itself, but in the Congo's case there was another need for educated women. The growing body of évolués were finding it increasingly difficult to marry women whose outlook on many aspects of life was very different from their own. This often created friction within the family, and in the upbringing of children caused uncertainty as to which parent should be followed.

Free Press

The question of a free press has been a serious one in the Congo. Under the Belgian colonial administration the press was not free. The Colonial Charter of 1908 recognized certain civil rights; and the freedom of the press, individual freedom, freedom of religion, freedom of opinion, freedom of education, inviolability of the home, the right to petition, the secrecy of private correspondence, the right of legal action against public officials, the inviolability of private property, and freedom of employment, were all recognized, at least in writing. But the right of meeting and freedom of the press was never really granted. The Belgian propaganda machine, a publication known as *Inforcongo*, comments somewhat lamely that "press censorship does not exist, but in the interior of the Congo the printing of some publication is subordinated to a system of authorizations, also subject to repeal. For reasons of public order, the authorities may also refuse the entry of certain foreign publications into the Congo." [1]

This control of freedom of the press was used by the colonial government to suppresss political activities and their legitimate organs of expression. The first Abako periodical, *Notre Kongo*, was seized on October 29, 1959, whereas other weekly publications had been forbidden as early as August, 1957. Nevertheless, the Congolese had grown increasingly conscious of the important part the press could play in mobilizing and molding public opinion in the country to support their cause. This was particularly true during the five years prior to independence. They were therefore prepared to fight for it. The attitude taken by the political leaders is well illustrated in Joseph Kasavubu's inaugural address in Leopoldville on April 20, 1958. He said:

> There is surveillance which is systematically exercised over our budding press. We protest energetically against this inhuman attitude and demand the immediate liberation of the native press. Our counsellors must understand that confidence is never gained gratuitously. It must be earned and merited.[2]

The concern which Congolese intellectuals like Thomas Kanza showed over these uncalled-for restrictions is indicated in speeches and writings appearing as early as 1959. Commenting on the suppression of the weekly publication *Congo*, Thomas Kanza wrote:

> The ordinance by which the authorization to publish was taken away from the founders-directors of *Congo* gave no justification. It was arbitrary and conformed to the colonial law. Sole master after God, he who held the power to give authorization to publish a journal was, in the Congo, the same who had the liberty to take it away when he wished and when it pleased him. The authorities forgot, however, that for the Africans, the conclusion was evident; the motive of this serious governmental measure could not be discussed. The paper was banned because the truths of colonial reality are not to be published or divulged—they are simply to be borne with joys and smiles. This suppression was a grave political error for the Belgians and a mistake which fell to the profit of the Congolese in their struggle for emancipation.[3]

But the Belgian government could not change its mind. The passage of several decrees in September, 1959, was a clear indication of the determination of the government to avoid dissemination by African leaders to their followers of political propaganda through their only legitimate organ —the press. A decree was signed by the King, stipulating that any person publishing a periodical must give prior notice in writing to the Provincial Governor. He must state the name of the periodical, its objectives, aims, board of directors or managers, and a precise list of the editorial staff. The governor of a province or his delegate was authorized to prohibit the introduction and circulation within the Congo of written material in any language which might in his judgment compromise the public order. These measures were not only meant to be preventive, but were also enforced. This is indicated by the enumeration of the penalties which applied to the infringement of the decree. All previous legislation regarding freedom of the press was abrogated accordingly. Despite these stringent restrictions, there were several newspapers circulated in the Congo. By 1955 the number of indigenous Congolese journalists began to increase. It was said that by this time about 400 publications were being circulated in the Congo, half of them newspapers. The radio and other media of communication remained strictly under state control.

Suppression of Political Activities

Most évolués lived in the urban areas, especially in the major cities—Leopoldville, Elizabethville, Stanleyville, and Coquilhatville. They had fairly good contacts with each other, and had opportunities to discuss their problems, hopes, and aspirations. But no political parties were allowed to be formed until recently. The Africans had no legitimate means of expressing their views directly to the central government. Even if the requests of the Africans reached the government, they could not be assured that the government would take action to remedy the complaints. This situation inevitably made the Congolese more politically conscious. It would be only through political action that the Congolese could bring about the changes that they desired. As this increasing awareness of political awakening was progressing, an important event occurred. In July, 1956, Joseph van Bilsen, a Belgian newspaperman and a lecturer at one of the Universities in Belgium who had spent a couple of years in the Congo, wrote an article that represented the first attempt by a Belgian to look at the Congo from the Congolese point of view. Van Bilsen disputed the official assumption that the Congolese must be raised gradually to civilized status before they could be given any responsibility for governing themselves. He urged Belgium to plan deliberately for self-government by promptly training Congolese leaders and administrators and pushing them up the ladder of government. This is something like what the British colonial policy has favored. Van Bilsen warned that "if we have no plans worthy of confidence, we will encounter, within fifteen to twenty years, maybe earlier, tensions and irrepressible movements." Most important of all, Van Bilsen proposed a time limit. This was done for the first time in the history of Belgian colonial policy. He entitled the article, "A Thirty Year Plan for the Emancipation of Belgian Congo."[4] He was the first to recognize and state clearly that there was a very important difference between ruling the Belgian Congo and being there to help the Congolese.

This article by Van Bilsen was immediately followed by manifestoes published by Africans.[5] The Abako, started as a socio-cultural organization in 1950, and soon after 1955, when Joseph Kasavubu became its president, turned into a political organization, made the essence of their platform as follows: "We want our political rights and all liberties NOW." The last word marked a significant break with the Belgian policy of gradualism.

About the same time, Patrice Lumumba's Liberal Club for increased political activity was started. First foundations of political consciousness were laid in the Congo. Nobody would have believed at this time that political freedom would be attained within five years.

Meanwhile, in 1955, the magic word, "self-government," was heard in the Congo, introduced very dramatically by none other than King Baudouin himself. He endorsed the Buisseret-Petillon program of improving the relations between the Africans and the Europeans. In a public address he said:

> I want to insist on the fact that the basic problem which now exists in the Congo is that of human relationships between black and white. It is not enough to equip the country materially, to endow it with wise social legislation, and to improve the standard of living of its inhabitants; it is imperative that the whites and the natives should show the widest mutual understanding in their daily contacts. The time will come—when exactly cannot yet be determined—to give our African territories a statute which will ... give to everyone, white and black, his part, according to merit and capacity in the government of the country.

Petillon, the Governor General of the Congo, amplified his ideas on the subject in a speech to his advisory council in 1956. He would begin by having popular elections for certain of the local positions and by generally educating the masses in politics. This would be followed by opening higher political positions to the Africans, and finally giving responsibility to them. He said, "Our ambition is not to sanction democracy in this country, but to introduce it and give it body little by little."

The new Congo politics soon clashed with Petillon's policy of gradualism. In 1957 certain towns were divided into communes, each of which would elect its own communal council, which in turn would choose a *bourgemestre* who would be then nominated by the Provincial Governor if he so desired. All males over twenty-five were allowed to vote. In December, 1957, the people of the six biggest cities went to the polls to vote for local councilors and *bourgemestres*. Most of the voting was on tribal lines. In five cities the elections were unorganized politically—they were contested by popular personalities. But in Leopoldville the Abako party, committed to self-government, waged a hard campaign, winning 60 per cent of the council seats in the native communes. Kasavubu became burgomaster of Dendale Commune. In his inaugural address, four months later, Kasavubu demanded immediate Congolese autonomy. He attacked the Belgian policy in the Congo. He was the first Congolese to do so. "For a country with 13 million inhabitants, we have 125 university students. We must wonder why the government has not used all its national and international possibilities after the War for the cultural development of the Congolese."

The Belgians were caught absolutely unprepared. They did not know what to do. Petillon with his assistants sat for several days wondering what to do. They couldn't do much. Kasavubu got away with an "official rebuke."

About this time in 1958, national elections were held in

Belgium and the Catholic party came into power. Van
Hemelrijck was named the new Minister for the Congo.
He was the first Minister to recognize Congolese political
sentiment. He realized the need to follow a new policy
in the Congo. With the coming of Van Hemelrijck, Belgian paternalism finally came to an end. He sought out
Congolese leaders and listened to them. His speeches
vaguely echoed Congolese demands. He was only being
realistic. It was he who gave permission to Lumumba
to attend the Accra Conference.

Hence by 1958 circumstances had forced Belgians
to give much greater political freedom to the Congolese
than they ever had before.

III

Now as to the Belgian policy of race relationship in the
Congo. This, as said earlier, is one of the most emotional
and important areas, which must be carefully examined.
Africans view racial discrimination as the acid test of the
intentions of the Europeans. They demand that the color
bar be declared illegal and a criminal offense punishable
by law. Dr. Kiano, former Minister of Commerce and
Industry of Kenya, once said that the word "black" has
been degraded so much that it is going to be the task of
the emerging African countries to change this derogatory
connotation and instead make the word one that will be respected. A part of Dr. Nnamdi Azikiwe's inaugural
speech when he became the Governor General will illustrate the African view on the subject. He said:

> Nigeria cannot concede it is in its national interest to
> fraternize with countries that practice race prejudice.
> We must not acquiesce in such an outrageous insult
> on the black race. Until the conscience of the world

has been energetically aroused to solve this problem frankly with absolute honesty, it is safe to predict that the political resurgence which is now sweeping all over Africa is capable of leading to a revanchist movement which would be disastrous to the peace of the world. We are bound to take cognizance of a situation where a minority, on account of its superior organization and influence, can usurp power and proceed to bully its majority population to the point of seeking to subdue them by sheer brute force.[6]

Racial prejudice has greatly violated the writings of a great man, who once wrote:

Man's dearest possession is life, and since it is given him to live but once, he must so live as not to be smeared with the shame of a cowardly existence and a trivial past, so live that dying he might say: all my life and all my strength were given to the finest cause in the world—the liberation of mankind.

Ever since 1885, the masters of the Congo had announced again and again that their intention was to build a true Belgian-Congolese partnership, but nothing substantial had been done to further this aim. It was only in 1954 when Premier Van Acker took office in Belgium that his Minister for the Colonies, August Buisseret, took some liberal measures. He started by trying to break down the color bar. Besides the attempt to assimilate certain numbers of Africans to the status of Europeans in the Congo, an effort was made to alleviate the growing discontent of the évolués by the gradual suppression of the distinction between black and white in the colony's legislation. Certain rights, which were formerly exclusively for the Europeans, were now extended to the Africans. Congolese were permitted to remain in the European sectors of cities until ten at night, and generally restrictions on freedom of movement were lifted or relaxed. In 1954 all Africans, whether "immatricules" or not, were empowered to become landowners, both in the "centres extra-coutumiers" and in the rural areas, where they could therefore theoretically become colons in the same way as the Europeans. In 1955 the Congolese were given rights to buy alcoholic drinks of all kinds and not just beer. They were allowed to drink in European-run cafés. An effort was made to unify the penal legislation for both the races. Similar attempts were made in the economic sphere where the Africans were gradually given the same privileges as the Europeans. Hence by 1951 family allowances were granted to Africans as well, and by 1956 an old age pension and health insurance were introduced. In trade union matters the Africans were finally given the right to strike in 1957.

There was no overnight social revolution, but at least a start was made toward removing some of the potentially explosive native grievances. Legal rights are, however, not sufficient to banish an uncomfortable feeling of not being wanted, and in practice economic barriers were such that even when there was no ban in theory, there existed one in practice. The main problem was not going to be solved by legislation, but rather by changing the minds of the people, as Governor General Jungers declared when he opened the Council de Gouvernement in 1949: "It is not possible to conceive of a country where there is no social hierarchy. But when the present evolution reaches its full development, this hierarchy must be based solely on differences of competence, of efficiency and of education."

In the postwar years it was the question of salaries that dominated the Africans' view regarding racial discrimination. They argued that what good are the official pronouncements about creating a true Belgo-Congolese community when there remained such great differences between the rates of pay of the Europeans and the Africans doing the same jobs. Even when an African had identical qualifications to a European he would be paid less than the European. This was not only true of the private sector of the economy, but also of the government administration. There is no excuse for the government to have different scales of pay. The private sector of the economy cannot be forced completely to follow the same policies as that of the government, but the government can erase racial discrimination by legislation.

Before the war, the spheres of African and European work were quite distinct and there were no complaints that racial prejudice existed. But after the war Africans and Europeans often did the same type of job, and in these cases discrimination in salaries was rightly shown as evidence of racial discrimination. The demand for equal pay for equal work became more and more general among the Africans. By 1958 the first group of graduates from Lavanium were ready. They wrote a letter to the Congolese administration demanding that there be no discrimination between white and black in the economic sphere. They received no reply; so they wrote an open letter to the Minister for the Congo, reminding him that he had promised that there would be no racial discrimination and that he should act to see that this promise of his was fulfilled. Due to the increasing pressure, it was legally pronounced that there would be no racial discrimination in the government administration. The private sector would soon follow the lead given by the government.

But this was not the end of the problem. One of the foundations for the equal pay for equal work clause was the opportunity for the Africans to gain the same qualifications as the Europeans. This meant equal opportunity in education, and hence the postwar insistence on higher education can be easily understood. Africans demanded educational opportunities equal to the Europeans. Until recently there were two entirely different educational systems: one very excellent system for the minority of European children, and another for the African majority. There were no multiracial schools. But in 1948 the strict racial basis of schools was broken down when schools which were formerly exclusively for the Europeans were opened to Asiatic children and to some of the children of mixed blood. By 1950 there was no legal barrier to interracial education in the Congo.

There still remained distinction for the races. Although students of all races could attend any school, the African children were examined not only in their educational qualifications but also their general background. The acceptance committee of the school would consider things like the income bracket of the child's family, his personal character, his health and cleanliness. This meant that there was still some discrimination. If the school wished to refuse any one student, it could do so. Often parents would be told that their child was not acceptable on grounds of health, but then when the parents went to the hospital they would be told that their child was not ill enough to need medical care. This was resented by the parents, and in 1958 there occurred a number of protests against this kind of practice in Elizabethville.[7]

IV

Before the Second World War the Belgians had managed to present a solid front to the Congolese. They made the Africans believe that there was no disagreement among the Belgians. But after the war this position changed. The all-powerful alliance of the "trinity"—the administration, the Catholic missions, and the companies—weakened. It was finally destroyed in 1954 when the newly elected Socialist-Liberal coalition took power in Brussels. The Africans realized that divisions existed in the domestic politics of Belgium and that they should make use of these divisions for their own benefit.

The main issue that brought out the differences between the state and the Church was the educational policy of the new administration. The mission had a virtual monopoly of education, though in 1946 some lay schools had been started for Europeans. When Buisseret became Minister for the Congo, he started lay schools for the Africans as well. He wanted to see that Africans too could send their children to nonprofessional schools. He set up a committee to inquire into the system of Catholic schools, and this report not only criticized but also ridiculed the Catholic educational system. The Minister reported that he was going to set up lay schools for Africans, and, more important, cut a very significant proportion of the subsidies to Catholic schools. The Catholic missionaries were furious and threatened to strike. The companies favored the Church because they feared that by the new policy the old alliance of the "trinity" would be destroyed and the Congo would be deprived of stability. The newspapers took sides for or against the new policy. The Governor General uttered a warning that the domestic politics of Belgium should not enter the Congo's affairs. "In the Congo we should not start to scorn and hate each other. We ought not to allow the inhabitants of the country—I am especially thinking of the natives—to be led to false conflicts, nor enlisted in factions . . ."

But the Africans were not so naive as to fail to recognize the opportunity they had to gain a great deal by this breakdown of the traditional alliance of the "trinity." Buisseret was hailed as a great liberator by the Congolese. In his defense of his policy the Minister for the Congo said that his policy was supported by African opinion, that he was setting up lay schools "in reply to the pressure of hundreds of Africans who speak in the name of various groups, as my documentation can show."

Belgian hope of maintaining the solid alliance of the "trinity" had failed.

V

The administration of the Congo was too centralized. The Belgian Government was aware of the general climate of resentment by the évolués of the paternalistic policies and the racial discrimination that existed in the Congo. But what the Belgians were not aware of was the degree of this resentment, and that this ill feeling on the part of the évolués was constantly growing at an increasing rate. The actions that the Belgians took were those that only relieved the pain temporarily, but they did not cure the illness completely. These policies were shortsighted. They just touched the surface of the problem. This is not strange, as few people were aware of the situation that existed in the Congo. Even those settlers who had lived there for their entire lives were not familiar with the forces that existed within the African community, especially the force of the évolués. Thus it was not surprising that when Petillon, former Governor General of the Belgian Congo and later in the Government of Prime Minister Eyskens as the Minister of the Congo, organized a study group of eminent Belgians to visit the country and make recommendations

about its future, Belgians wondered why a man who had
spent the whole of his life in the Congo would send a
study group to find what was happening there. But Petillon
knew better. There was something going on in the Congo,
for which even his long experience in the Congo had not
prepared him, and that the Belgians would be even more
unprepared to face. The study group privately reported
that the deadline for independence had to be advanced by
more than half of the limit which Van Bilsen had suggested.
This was unexpected news to most Belgians.

Soon after this the serious Leopoldville riots occurred,
between January 4-7, 1959. The significance of these riots
in the political history of the Congo can hardly be over-
emphasized. This was the first serious indication to the
colonial authorities, both in the Congo and Belgium, that
the "wind of change" blowing throughout Africa was no
ordinary wind, but a raging hurricane. Even the Portuguese, who for a long time thought that they would not
be affected by the ominous trend of this hurricane, have
at last tasted its political force and moral strength. It has
been suggested that the Leopoldville riots were triggered
by Patrice Lumumba's so-called fiery speech in the commune of Kalamu in Leopoldville before a crowd of 7,000
people. Lumumba had just returned from the Conference
of All-African Peoples held in Accra, Ghana, in the month
of December, 1958. Both the Abako Party leaders and
Movement National Congolaise leaders had been invited,
but only the three members of MNC—Patrice Lumumba,
the President, Joseph Ngalula, editor of *Presence Congolaise*, and Gaston Diomi, burgomaster of the Ngiri-Ngiri
Commune of Leopoldville—attended. Joseph Kasavubu, the
President of Abako Party, failed to make any appearance.
The reason for his failure to attend the conference was not

clearly established, but it was said that he had certain difficulties with his inoculation certificates. It can not be said
that the Belgian colonial authorities placed any obstacles
in his way because they adopted a very co-operative attitude with the political leaders in the Congo so that all
should have been plain sailing insofar as the acquisition of
permits to Accra was concerned.

The three leaders who had attended the Accra meeting
were accorded cordial treatment by the hospitable Ghan-
aians and other members of the Conference. Lumumba and
his followers saw for the first time the African personality
in its real context. Many delegates from all over the continent demanded total decolonization and emancipation of
the still remaining colonial territories in Africa. The Congo
was no longer an isolated country. The Congolese leaders
heard the chairman of the Conference, Mr. Tom Mboya,
tell the colonial powers to "scram from Africa." Instead
of the scramble for Africa which took place after the
Berlin Conference in 1885, a clarion call had been issued
by the indigenous Africans for the reverse to take place.
The President of the Republic of Ghana, and host to the
delegates, the Osagyefo Dr. Kwame Nkrumah, made the
following speech to the delegates:

> Ghana supports the struggle of the dependent peoples
> for the speedy determination of imperialism and
> colonialism and the eradication from this continent of
> racialism. As I have always declared, even before
> Ghana attained her present sovereign status, "the
> independence of Ghana will be meaningless unless it
> is linked up with the total liberation of Africa." We
> have not moved from this premise nor shall we budge
> one jot from it until the final goal has been reached
> and the last vestiges of imperialism and colonialism

have been wiped off this African continent. We disdain to hide these aims and objectives of ours. We proclaim them freely to the world. We have pride in our determination to support every form of nonviolent action which our fellow Africans in colonial territories may find fit to use in the struggle for their legitimate rights and aspirations. We make no apology to anyone, and we will not allow ourselves to be deflected from this just cause, a cause wholly in consonance with the principles enunciated in the Charter of the United Nations.[8]

Lumumba was made a member of the permanent secretariat set up at the Conference. He had contacts for the first time with other prominent African leaders who greatly impressed him. During the Conference he made a short speech in which he gave a resumé of the political developments in the Congo to that date, December 11, 1958. He pronounced his party's policy to be the liberation of the Congolese people from the colonial regime and their accession to independence, and cited the United Nations Declaration of Human Rights to be the basis of his demand. He scored Belgium's colonial policy and strongly condemned any move to Balkanize the Congo. Lumumba closed with: "Down with colonialism and imperialism! Down with racism and tribalism! Long live the Congolese nation; long live independent Africa."[9]

It is probable that on his return to Leopoldville Lumumba greatly increased his political activities. Before this he was not on good terms with Kasavubu, but they were publicly reconciled after his return from Accra. The speech which has been said to have caused the riots was made on December 28, 1958, just prior to the riots. His ability to stir up a crowd and his unenviable record of sowing riot and dissent in many parts of the Congo were attributed to the Leopoldville riots. Nevertheless, some observers argue that there was no connection at all between Lumumba's "fiery speech" and the Leopoldville riots. Hence the frequent consideration of other possible causes. The most important among these was the tension due to chronic unemployment. (For details on this particular issue, see Alan P. Merriam, *Congo: Background of Conflict*, pp. 84-86). Since the actual riots occurred, there has been so much differing statistical information given as to the number of casualties sustained, that it is difficult to establish with complete accuracy. Many people give their own version of the story, but I think a total of at least seventy people were killed.[10]

The Belgian Government received the news with grim silence and regarded it as a national disaster. The thought of another Algeria occurred to many people as a possibility, and none was prepared to welcome such a costly colonial war. This was the time to be liberal about independence demands or never. The entire country was panicked about the rapid political consciousness of the hitherto unconcerned Congolese people. But in actual fact the Congolese people had not been unconcerned at all with their plight. The colonial system had for a long time failed to reaffirm faith in fundamental human rights, in the dignity and worth of the human person, and in the equal rights of men and women and of nations large and small to establish conditions under which justice and respect for the obligations arising from treaties and other sources of international law could be maintained. Bad as the Berlin Conference Treaty was for the cause of African freedom, it was made worse by Leopold II's failure to observe the obligations of the treaty to protect African natives in the Congo. There were other aspects which were bound to backfire. Failure by the colonial powers to promote social progress and better standards of life in larger freedom for the African people bred a potentially dangerous situation.

Therefore, on January 13, the Government issued its declaration that democracy would be instituted in the Congo as soon as possible. King Baudouin said:

> Our firm resolution today is to lead the Congolese population, without harmful procrastination, but also without thoughtless haste, toward independence in prosperity and peace.

NOTES: *Chapter 5*

1. Anonymous: "Thirteen Million Congolese," Bruxelles; *Inforcongo* n.d. 79 pp. (see p. 69)
2. Demany, Fernand: *S.O.S. Congo* (Chronique d'un Soulévement), Bruxelles: Editions Labour, 1959, p. 167
3. Merriam, A.P., *Congo: Background of Conflict*, p. 53
4. A.A.J. Van Bilsen, "Un plan de trente ans pour l'emancipation politique de l'Afrique Belge," in "Les dossiers de l'Action sociale catholique," Brussels, Feb. 1956
5. Ref. to Chapter 4, *Conscience Africain*
6. *Christian Science Monitor*, February 17, 1960
7. Ruth Slade, *The Belgian Congo, Some Recent Changes*, Institute of Race Relations (Oxford Univ. Press, 1960)
8. Tawia Adamafio: *Hands Off Africa—Some Famous Speeches by Dr. Kwame Nkrumah*, published by Kwebena Owusu-Akyem, Ministry of Local Government, P.O. Box M.50, Accra.
9. Demany, Fernand: *op. cit.*, pp. 162-172
10. Merriam, Alan P., *op. cit.*, p. 87

CHAPTER 6

The Commission of Inquiry

AFTER THE JANUARY DISTURBANCES OF 1959 in Leopoldville and other parts of the Congo which resulted in about seventy deaths, the Belgian Government realized that African nationalism in the Congo had reached its peak and that something had to be done to avoid further bloodshed. Furthermore, the government's policy in the Congo had to be declared very soon, otherwise serious trouble was sure to follow. Nothing could have stopped the surging aspirations of the Congolese people. M. Van Hemelrijck's progressive policy in the Congo had a chance now to be put into operation. It would seem that the riots were instrumental in rallying the government, although with much hesitation, to this progressive policy. But before the announcement of the government policy, King Baudouin's radio message preceded it. The King said that "it is our firm intention, without undesirable procrastination but also without undue haste, to lead the Congolese populations forward towards independence in prosperity and peace."

On July 1, 1885, Belgium recognized the Congo Independent Free State as a personal property of King Leopold II. Twenty-three years later, on October 18, 1908, the Belgian Government took over the administration of the state, thereby making it a colony of the metropolitan country. On June 30, 1960, the colony became a completely free and independent republic. The Congo took her place in the community of nations and with a voice that was soon to echo all over the globe. No one could have foreseen that in the space of seventy-five years the Congo would change from an almost unknown spot on the African map to a country standing in the center of the spotlights that illuminate the current contest between East and West. Yet the movements for decolonization and complete political emancipation of the Congo cannot be traced throughout those seventy-five years with ease; the actual increased political tempo in the country did not really take hold until 1955. Before that time there was only a confused colonial policy administered by Belgians, although it can be said that some tentative beginnings of African participation in government began as early as 1947. In that year, two Congolese nations were appointed to the governmental Council which hitherto had been the exclusive preserve of the Europeans. Things progressed in such a way that by 1951 the interests of Africans were cared for by the government appointment of eight African members. Such small things provided further political advancement of the Africans until, in 1957, some local governments were elected by African people.

Developments in the field of education also began during the early fifties.[1] Mr. Thomas Kanza, who later became the first Congolese ambassador to the United Nations in the Lumumba government, was sent to a university in Belgium. Our discussions with Kanza in New York City and later at Harvard University where he had been invited by the author to address a meeting at Quincy House, revealed the fact that he was the first Congolese student to be sent abroad to pursue further education. There followed in 1953 a group of fifteen Congolese drawn from all of the six provinces of the country who were taken to Brussels for an extensive tour and shown all aspects of Belgian life, of which they had had very little idea. In fact, two of these men were later appointed by Mr. Lumumba to his cabinet, while several of them figured prominently in independent movements.[2]

In 1955 when King Baudouin visited the Congo, the people were greatly awakened as to their political future. It was estimated that on the first leg of his visit in Leopoldville he was met by a crowd of 200,000 Africans and 15,000 Europeans. His tour of the state took him to such Congolese towns as Usumbura, Bukavu, Stanleyville, Coquilhatville, Luluabourg, Kamina, Kolwevi, Elizabethville, Tadotville, and the three main cities of Ruanda-Urundi. The latter country has been administered by the Belgian Government under the trusteeship system agreement according to Chapter 13, Article 86 of the United Nations Charter. It was reported that everywhere the King went he was enthusiastically greeted and welcomed by the people, and the Africans in particular gave him loud cheers and acclaim which symbolized rising hopes and expectations,[3] with regard to their political aspirations. In fact, certain European experts on the Congo observe that for the Congolese people, the Belgian King was not by any means the representative of Belgium, but was regarded by them as their own chief, "someone who was interested in their social welfare and in the difficulties of their daily lives." That he appeared to the Congolese "in the form of a Liberator who would put the Europeans in their place, sweep away the social barriers dividing white and black, and usher in a happier state of affairs." And for these reasons it was thus a bitter disappointment to many to find that all did not immediately change after his visit.[4]

There was disappointment. Nevertheless, the Congolese politicians were rather skeptical of getting any immediate political reforms without a vanguard political party agitating for them. It would be a complete misunderstanding of the African people to say that they have ever expected somebody to hand them freedom and independence on a silver platter. On the contary, the African has many times categorically stated that independence must be the result of the people's struggle. A clear example can be seen in the speech below by Patrice Lumumba to the Congolese people on December 28, 1958, after his return from the All-African People's Conference in Accra, Ghana:

> The Conference demands immediate independence for all Africa and that no country in Africa remain under foreign domination after 1960. We state with satisfaction that the resolutions of the Conference coincide with the views of our movement. The independence that we claim in the name of peace cannot be considered any longer by Belgium as a gift, but to the contrary, it is a right that the Congolese peoples have lost. The objective is to unite and organize the Congolese masses in the struggle for amelioration of their lot, the liquidation of the colonial regime and the exploitation of man by man. It is high time that the Congolese people prove to the world that they are cognizant of the realities of the "autonomy gift" which the government is preparing and promising. We don't want this autonomy. The Congolese people must stop sleeping and waiting for our independence and liberty. The Congo is our country. It is our duty to make it greater and better.[5]

The above speech shows the complete break between the Congolese nationalists like Lumumba, who demanded immediate and unconditional independence on the basis of complete equality, and the Belgian King, who made tentative gestures toward political evolution and offered the usual talk about strengthening relations between Belgians and Congolese and about the emergence of a joint Belgo-Congolese state. This latter item was a multiracial society which the British advocated in Kenya but failed to produce, and which is still being touted by settlers of European origin in Southern Rhodesia in particular, but also in Northern Rhodesia and Nyasaland. The concept of a joint Belgo-Congolese state as advanced by Belgium is set forth by Ruth Slade in the following terms:

> The time will then come—the date cannot yet be determined—to give our African territories a status which will guarantee, for the happiness of all, the continuing existence of a true Belgo-Congolese community, and which will assure to each, white or black, his proper share in the country's government, according to his own qualities and capacity. Before we realize this high ideal, Gentlemen, much remains to be done.[6]

The futility of such a view was not only apparent in the Congo, but already had been fully proven in the Federation of Rhodesia and Nyasaland, Kenya, South Africa, and the Portuguese territories of Angola and Mozambique where we find a large concentration of European settler groups. The emphasis is not on independence for the Africans but on a joint Belgo-Congolese community meant for all practical purposes to be the perpetuation of colonialism. In such a community the responsibilities and rewards would for many years inevitably rest with the Belgians. It is not unfair to point out that for many years the Europeans in Africa have found it politically expedient to mention very carefully that a state or society would some-how be created in which white and black would "share in the country's government according to . . . qualities and capacity," for the sole purpose of perpetuating European domination. How can any European politician argue that "much remains to be done" before the Africans are given responsible positions in the government, without even em-barking on the most fundamental and modest political, economic, and social reforms? What is normally done is that no political promises are made, no timetables for inde-pendence created; rather, there is always just a grain of hope that given the proper circumstances and enough time, something will be done about Africa and its political evolution. We Africans consider this stand to be no stand at all. In the case of the Congo, this attitude, typical of the cautious and tentative Belgian nature, was clearly seen when it became apparent how little thought had been given by mid-1955 to the Congo as an independent state.

In Central Africa, European leaders like Sir Roy Welen-sky and Sir Edgar Whitehead are the champions of white supremacy and white civilization in Africa. They often regard African leaders as power-hungry extremists and racialists inspired by a completely irresponsible and vicious nationalism. The government of South Africa under the leadership of Dr. Hendrik Verwoerd stands for an even more obnoxious racialist policy, which is bound to end up in a catastrophic explosion unless the downward avalanche to apartheid is quickly arrested. One of the blindest aspects of the doctrine of white supremacy in Africa is the belief that the African is a different type of human being, that he is not the same as those elsewhere in the world—subject to reason and prejudice, to feelings of sympathy and revenge, selfishness and self-sacrifice.

Moreover, it is hardly recognized that contrary to accusations by European leaders of African racialism, our only opposition to the classification of any African state as a multiracial state stems from the fact that what we want is a society where the individual matters, and not the color of his skin or the shape of his nose. Racial group privileges or discriminations are manifestly incompatible with this aim. The institution of a nonracial democratic society is our main objective, and any success or failure toward this goal will be largely dictated by the attitude adopted by white supremacists in our midst. The creation of an atmosphere of interracial harmony can never be attained in a society where there is a high correlation between income and race. What is more, a legacy of interracial suspicion and all that accompanies it mocks the whole concept of fundamental equality.

The Congo "disaster" can hardly be understood without considering the problems of race and color in African politics. As we have seen, toward the end of 1955 the situation in the Congo was deceptively calm, unbroken by almost any suggestion of independence for the Congo or even of any concrete thinking about future plans and aims. The only criticism of the Belgian government's policy in the Congo came from a Belgian professor, forty-six-year old A. A. M. Van Bilsen, who was then at the University Institute for Overseas Territories in Antwerp. As mentioned, Professor Bilsen published his thirty-year plan for the political emancipation of the Belgian Congo.[7] His plan actually contained no specific terms, but he was very precise about the lack of firm and clear directives from the metropole, which had resulted in the colony being ruled and developed without following any predetermined line or doctrine for which the Belgian Parliament could take responsibility and for which it would be accountable to the local electorate. He also pointed out the absence of any Congolese being trained in the high offices of the government for eventual take-over from Belgium. This, as we know, has been greatly criticized by all nations. Van Bilsen wrote: "It is our fault, not theirs [the Congolese] that there are no doctors, veterinarians, engineers, functionaries or officers among them," and he compared this attitude with that of the progressive missionaries who had apparently trained quite a few native priests and bishops. He pointed out also the unbalanced growth of industrialization in the country.

In fact, Professor Van Bilsen's view that the traditional fault of colonial authorities is that they make concessions only when they can no longer do otherwise is one of the classic criticisms of colonialism. To give too little too late reflects lack of any historical awareness of nationalism by the authorities. The Belgians gave too little attention not only to the formation of a competent indigenous civil service but also to the awakening among the people of a sense of responsibility and political activity toward the general good. It is therefore interesting to note that the above-mentioned reasons prompted Professor Van Bilsen to believe that it would take thirty years before the Congolese people could be prepared to shoulder the burdens of independence. The quotation below is illustrative of Van Bilsen's attitude on unrehearsed independence.

> In the Congo and Ruanda-Urundi the formation of elite and of responsible directing cadres is a generation behind the British and French territories. In thirty years, the children born between now and 1960 will form the active base of the population. Among the elites, the youngest will have completed their uni-

versity studies or their preliminary education. What the Congo will be in thirty years will be the function of what we do between now and 1960 and 1965. If we wish it, in a generation our African territories will be in a position to take their proper destiny in their own hands. It is our duty and in our interests to see that this is done. If we do not create and execute a plan, we will not be able to do what is necessary in time. If we do not have a plan, in fifteen or twenty years, if not before, we will find ourselves faced by tensions and irresistible movements in several parts of our territories.[8]

What Professor Van Bilsen advocated six years ago was to become the practical thing in 1960. The fact that at this point he also proposed "a grand Congolese Federation" is striking enough, since this is one of the remaining unresolved political questions in the Congo. Van Bilsen's arguments on a Congolese Federation rested on the facts that the physical size of the state rendered the workability of a centralized government virtually impossible; that Ruanda-Urundi were too weak economically to stand on their own feet after independence, and finally, that a federal system of government was in conformity with the already created pattern by the Belgian colonial authorities. The latter argument was erroneous because under the Belgian colonial administration the Congo had a centralized government with headquarters in Leopoldville. There was no local autonomy with the six provinces comprising the Republic. Nevertheless, the federal issue was later to appear as one of the chief bones of contention in the Congo before and after independence, as we shall later see.

In effect, Van Bilsen's plan drew the attention of the Belgian government to the immediate need for a wise and deliberate plan to introduce political, economic, and social reforms in the Congo. The enormity of Belgium's task was squarely faced and some practical suggestions were made. With the colonial mentality prevailing in Brussels during that period it was easy to predict accurately the Belgian response to these suggestions. Mr. Raymond Scheyven was hardly enthusiastic, since he opposed any timetable being set for the Congo's eventual decolonization.

> I see a danger in fixing a time limit. How can one say to a capitalist, a technician, "Come and settle down, invest your money, your energy, and your intelligence, but look out, in ten, twenty, or thirty years, your time will be ended." How can you encourage a young man to come and work in the Congo if you tell him at the same time that he hasn't even before him the time to make a full career.[9]

This attitude clearly reflects the inability of the Belgian authorities to understand Africa and the nationalist movements toward independence. Nationalism is like a flowing river, and nothing can stop it indefinitely from flowing. As late as 1957, the Belgian Minister of the Congo, Mr. Buisseret, spoke with great scorn of those "irresponsible strategists who fix dates" for Congolese independence. This is not to say, however, that all responses from Belgium to Professor Van Bilsen's proposals were a definite no. There were undoubtedly some liberal and progressive groups in the Socialist Party and the Roman Catholic Social Action Group who reacted quite favorably to the ideas.

With these developments in mind the Congolese people were profoundly affected by the King's declaration of 1960, because it laid the ground for universal adult suffrage in the election of members of the communal and territorial councils. It now became clear to the people that Belgium was prepared to accord independence to them, and was preparing the way for internal autonomy by a system of councils elected by universal adult suffrage, despite the fact that the declaration was as vague as it could be. The Belgians later conceded that complete independence would be granted by 1964, but this proved to be a mere dream, as we shall see. What was significant, though, was the fact that for the first time in the history of the Congo, Belgium had said that she intended to organize the Congo as a democracy, capable of exercising the prerogatives of sovereignty and of deciding the question of independence for itself. Some Europeans in the Congo were in sharp disagreement with the government's idea of according the Africans political freedom. They panicked, began to close down their shops, and formed a "committee for public safety." But these isolated incidents of opposition from the settler communities had no serious effects. The Africans were on the march toward the goal of attaining their political kingdom, and nothing in the Congo or Brussels was going to stop them. When the Minister of the Congo, M. Van Hemelrijck, toured the Congo, he did not receive a very enthusiastic welcome from the settlers although the Fedacol (the settlers' federation)was not as such unfavorable.

II

Before dealing with the Brussels Round Table Conference which took place January, 1960, to grant the Congo formal independence, let us consider the facts and recommendations contained in the Report of the Parliamentary Commission of Inquiry that went to the Congo after the riots of Leopoldville in January, 1959. The Parliamentary

Commission of Inquiry was composed of nine members. It arrived in Leopoldville four days after the rioting began. Their report produced later was honest and frank, and there is no question as to its impartiality. It completely discarded the propaganda, the pretense and deception and bogus claims about the advantages of paternalism over democratic political rights. The reports form a useful postscript for "multiracial" territories which might seek to profit from the mistakes made by Belgium in the Congo.

I say this because I think that the major political problem still facing Africa today is undoubtedly the self-deception of Europeans in multiracial areas such as Southern Rhodesia and South Africa. In those societies European supremacy is firmly maintained by an elaborate structure of propaganda both intentionally and unintentionally designed to reassure the white settlers of the justice of their cause, and to prevent the outside world from understanding what is really happening. It so happened that the Belgians in practice nearly succeeded at this in the Congo. They genuinely deceived themselves about the success of their own paternalist policies; they laid a massive smoke screen that prevented a proper assessment of the wide gaps between their claims and their achievements. Colin Legum, the correspondent on African affairs for the *London Observer*, has said: "Nobody achieved greater success in providing a rationale for their paternalism; moral fervor and intellectual argument were harnessed to their cause. Inforcongo—The Belgian Department of Information in the Congo—was one of the finest propaganda machines in the world; the only pity of it is that it was not put to any better use. But the efficiency of Belgian propaganda was a double-edged sword. For the awakening came with such shattering swiftness and force that it left the Belgians bewildered and aghast at their own self-deception."

The moment of truth, of course, came with the angry riots in Leopoldville on January 4, 1959. On January 8 the Belgian Parliament sent their Commission to discover what had gone wrong. We should note that King Baudouin's declaration of "leading the Congolese people to independence in prosperity and peace without fatal delays, but without inconsiderate haste," came out before the Commission's work was finished. The Commission was, therefore, compelled to discard any form of propaganda, including the pretense about the advantage of paternalism over democratic political rights. The Commission defined three stages in the evolution of a colony under white rule. I shall list them below in detail:

> 1. "The first phase follows on the period of occupation and pacification; the presence of the white man is accepted without discussion; he gives the orders and is obeyed. The rulers know their wishes."
>
> 2. In the second phase the white man's sense of responsibility for the black man grows weaker. "Blacks are increasingly looked upon as workers with no personality of their own; they must be educated and instructed, though chiefly to increase the value of their labor; they are turned into skilled workers and clerks. At this time, the whites in the larger centers have no other relations with the blacks than is necessary for their employment. The blacks make no complaints; they must submit themselves without opposition to the privileges enjoyed by the whites. But,

gradually as they become more efficient in their work, their intellectual vision rises and they begin to see things in a different light."

3. The third stage comes with the declaration of human rights and the emancipation of colonies. This becomes more difficult. "The whites are bound to a society in which the color of one's skin plays an important role; on the other hand, the black évolués seek the immediate eradication of color bars."

The Commission continues from this incisive analysis to consider the effects of deteriorating human relations. It shows how the whites at once became divided in their attitudes toward the new situation, most of them poisoning relations by their words and actions, thereby exacerbating the situation. The "small white" feels that the rise of African évolués threatens his social position by the likelihood of the évolués filling his lower-paid post. The "small white" at once assumes a superiority complex, unsoftened by psychological insight. The Commission then declares that "in a country where the white man is both judge and jury, it is human that the black man should begin to feel that he can get no justice because he is black."

Another cause of friction which the Commission dealt with was the disparity in wages. It said, "The individual feelings of vengeance and of grievance are progressively increased; daily the dissatisfaction rises and is exploited by the black leaders in whose interests it is to spread hate against the Europeans. At the first opportunity the hatred explodes."

It can be said in general that the Commission of Inquiry exposed a lot of hitherto hidden mistakes of the Belgian colonial administration in the country. Their findings are succinctly summed up in the chapter heading: "The Tardiness of the Authorities; the lack of decision, and the weakness of the Administration."

The report therefore put finis to the dangerous procrastination and illusions of the Belgians in their Congo policy. It also did a very important job by upholding the criticisms of those who for years had tried unsuccessfully to puncture the propaganda of *Inforcongo*—the Belgian propaganda publication in the Congo. The much-vaunted paternalism was proved to be both ineffective and deceptive. Those who had praised it came to lament it. Even the Prime Minister of Belgium, M. Gaston Eyskens, was reported as saying: "Indeed a political mistake was made in the past." But the unfortunate thing is that the mistake was discovered only atfer African nationalism had bolted from the stable.

Perhaps one of the most significant aspects of the findings of the Parliamentary Commission of Inquiry was their recommendation for the reorganization of the Congolese National Army and the police force.[10] The military intervention and the conduct during the riots caused deep concern to the Commission. Even later, when the Congo had been plunged into a deep crisis after independence on June 30, 1960, many responsible statesmen in the United Nations Security Council and General Assembly echoed this point. Notable among these was Mr. Kwame Nkrumah, the President of Ghana. The Commission made some recommendations with regard to this particular issue and provided the basis for possible future operations. It also discussed what should be done to prevent future outbreaks of a similar kind. The most important among these were the improvement of human relationships and the development of friendly relations among Africans and Europeans based on respect for the principle of equal rights and self-determination for everyone, and the practice of tolerance and living together in peace with one another as good neighbors. It was necessary at this stage to speed up the improvement of communications media, adopt a clear-cut long-range political policy for the Congo, modify the towns' electoral systems, establish a program to combat the chronic unemployment situation which had already reached almost unmanageable proportions, and establish a national labor council. An increase in educational facilities, long overdue, and the promotion of youth movements to provide the proper framework for increased political and social activities, were cited by the Commission as important.

Apart from the sending of the Commission to the Congo, the Belgian government took other measures to arrest what it considered to be a rapidly deteriorating political and social situation. The Abako political party was dissolved and its leaders arrested and detained without trial. Nevertheless, the Belgians eventually released some of the arrested leaders on March 14, 1959, among whom were Joseph Kasavubu (President), Daniel Kanza (the father of Thomas Kanza who later became the first Congolese Minister Extraordinary and Ambassador Plenipotentiary to the United Nations), and Simon Nzeza. On their release they were sent directly to Belgium where they arrived on March 17, 1959. Although they were allowed full liberty in Belgium and availed themselves of the opportunity to travel throughout the country, they were constantly under the strict surveillance of security guards. They were allowed to return to the Congo on May 13, 1959, almost two months later.[11]

The significance of the shipment of these political prisoners to Belgium has never been established although from the context one can make a good guess. If it were for the purpose of softening the demands of these leaders for political emancipation, I would venture to say that the objective was not realized. In effect the differences in colonial policy among the colonial powers here becomes apparent. The British, in the first place, would detain a political prisoner for several years as in the case of Jomo Kenyatta in Kenya (over eight years); or a few years only as in the case of Kwame Nkrumah of Ghana or Archbishop Makarios of Cyprus. But the Belgians only applied a three-month sentence without trial and no restriction order after the completion of the sentence. These matters also depend on several factors such as the dynamic character of the leader in question, the internal pressure of groups and external political considerations in the metropolitan country,[12] and the prevailing political atmosphere.

In the meantime, the Congo received the first governmental declaration as well as a message from the King concerning its future political status. This was on January 13, 1959. Much controversy has been engendered as to the wisdom and timing of these declarations. One school of thought advanced the argument that Belgium should have been a little tougher with the African nationalists while at the same time giving some political concessions. The argument that such an approach was rendered impossible by the Leopoldville riots has been questioned severely by certain scholars: "This seems to have no basis in fact, however, for it is clear that the pronouncements had long been planned for that particular date." I do not think it is unfair to say that no plan of this nature had been conceived by Belgium. Nothing dramatic had taken place in the thoughts of the ruling circles in Brussels to make them abandon their former reaction to Professor Van Bilsen's suggestions for a planned, coherent policy on the Congo. Moreover, Belgium's own reaction to the riots indicated that from that time on things were done in a great hurry and in a helter-skelter way. It is therefore completely untenable to suggest that there had been any plan. It is even more absurd to suggest that the Leopoldville riots had been planned for January 13, but got out of hand and therefore took place nine days earlier.[13] As Merriam indicates, and rightly too, "there has not been any proof of such a possibility." It is my submission that these riots were a spontaneous reaction by a frustrated people who believed in the nobility of the cause which they had embraced as just and wholly in consonance with the purpose and principles of the United Nations Charter. The year 1959 was the year of decision in the Congo. It was a question of either fighting or abdicating.

Now, the King's declaration was of great political significance, for it was the first official document that used the word independence. It said, *inter alia*:

> The aim of our presence on the dark continent has been defined by Leopold II: to open these backward countries to European civilization, to call their populations to emancipation, liberty and progress after having freed them from slavery, illness and misery. Our firm resolve without undesirable delays but also without inconsidered precipitation is to lead the Congolese people to independence in prosperity and peace. Far from imposing on these populations solutions which are entirely European, we shall favor original adaptations which respond to the proper character and traditions which are dear to them.

In the twinkling of an eye, the long-delayed reforms for

the Congo had been announced. In fact, no colonial power in history was destroyed more quickly, nor by such a rabble. Due to lack of serious concentrated political activity, there was not a very coherent nationalist movement which could command nation-wide support. But the fact remained that there was a serious rebellion; a rebellion of the mind that rejected paternalism and all it stood for. The children were children no longer. The Belgian government conceded that she intended to organize in the Congo a democracy capable of exercising its prerogatives of sovereignty and of deciding on its independence. As a co-signator of the United Nations Charter, she had, *ipso facto,* confirmed her wish to lead the people of the Congo to the point where they would be capable of governing themselves,[14] so that all her actions in the Congo were to be directed toward this line of conduct. The only tragedy is that she realized these things too late, for the Congo had been regarded by many colonial powers as the "blue chip colony." Pierre Wigny, the Belgian Foreign Minister, had once remarked that "is there a finer relationship than that which exists between father and child?" But he never realized that it takes two to maintain a true paternalist relationship. "When things go wrong between father and son, the parent must be capable of either tyranny or of changing his attitude; in either case the relationship changes."[15] But in the case of the Congo, when it came to the test the Belgians had no stomach for tyranny as we know it. They tried but failed to change their attitude; and they ended up muddled, defensive, resentful, and completely ineffectual.

NOTES: *Chapter 6*

1. Alan P. Merriam, *Congo—Background of Conflict,* (Northwestern University Press, 1961) pp. 66-67

2. See Anonymous, "Nous nous y sommes sentis chez-vous; notes de voyage des 15 notables Congolais qui visiterent la Belgique en 1953." (*Kalina*: Service de; 'Information, 1954, p. 254) Also see Freudenheim, Milt "U.S. Warns: We'll Shoot Russ in Congo," *Chicago Daily News*, 21 July 1960, page 1 paras. 1-2 and page 4, paras. 5-7

3. T. Gerard, *La Monarchie Belge Abandonnera-t-elle le Congo?* (Bruxelles: Editions Europe-Afrique, 1960), p. 95

4. Slade, Ruth, *The Belgian Congo: Some Recent Changes*, (London: Oxford University Press under the Institute of Race Relations, 1960), p. 55

5. Mendiaux, Edouard. *Moscou, Accra et le Congo.* Bruxelles: Charles Desart, 1960, p. 198

6. Slade, Ruth, *op. cit.*, pp. 19-20

7. Van Bilsen, A. A. J. "Vers L'Independance du Congo et du Ruanda-Urundi; Reflexions sur les Devoirs et L'Avenir de la Belgique en Afrique Centrale." Kraainem, pp. 164-202

8. Van Bilsen, *Ibid*, p. 176

9. Anonymous—"Independance Congolaise Pacifique Conquete," (Bruxelles, Editions de Remarques Congolaises, Collection *Etudes Congolaises No. 3*, 1960), p. 52

10. Note: With regard to the Parliamentary Commission of Inquiry, further reports could be found from: Anonymous, "Parliamentary Enquiry on the Troubles," *Inforcongo* April, 1959

11. Kanza, Thomas R. *Tot ou Tard* (Ata Ndele), (Bruxelles: Le Livre Africain, 1959) 85 pp. (See pp. 40-45)

12. It is said that in the case of Kenyatta, his release was a great subject of concern to the Conservatives (i.e. Right-Wing elements) in the British Parliament.

13. Merriam, A. P. *op. cit.*, p. 88

14. Article 73, Chapter XI, of the United Nations Charter regarding a declaration of non-self-governing territories states that "Members of the United Nations which have or assume responsibilities for the administration of territories whose peoples have not yet attained a full measure of self-government recognize the principle that the interests of the inhabitants of these territories are paramount, and accept as a sacred trust the obligation to promote to the utmost, within the system of international peace and security established by the present Charter, the well-being of the inhabitants of these territories, and, to this end:

    "(a) to insure, with due respect for the cultures of the peoples concerned, their political, economic, social, and educational advancement, their just treatment, and their protection against abuses;

    "(b) to develop self-government, to take due account of the political aspirations of the peoples, and to assist them in the progressive development of their free political institutions, according to the particular circumstances of each territory and its people and their varying stages of advancement;

"(c) to further international peace and security;

"(d) to promote constructive measures of development, to encourage research, and to co-operate with one another and, when and where appropriate, with specialized international bodies with a view to the practical achievement of the social, economic and scientific purposes set forth in this Article; and

"(e) to transmit regularly to the Secretary General for information purposes, subject to such limitations as security and constitutional considerations may require, statistical and other information of a technical nature relating to economic, social and educational conditions in the territories for which they are respectively responsible."

15. Legum, Colin: *Congo Disaster*, (Penguin Books, Baltimore, Maryland, 1961), p. 57.

CHAPTER 7

The Round Table Conference
and *Uhuru*-Independence

THE BELGIAN GOVERNMENT announced that it had revised its proposed timetable for the Congo's independence. The Belgians appeared to have accepted 1960 instead of the previous 1964 as the target date. There were increased riots in the Congo even after the King had toured the country. The Belgian Minister for the Congo, Auguste de Schryver, reviewing the King's tour of the Congo at a news conference on January 4, 1960 said: "There is only one unanimity among the Congolese. This is to demand independence. At the present moment, the Congo is rejoicing that the King has visited it. There is an easing of tension, but the problems remain."[1] At the same time, however, the tribal hostility between the Luluas and Balukas broke anew and several people were killed near Luluabourg. The author later visited Luluabourg and he saw several people who were critically wounded as a result of these tribal clashes. More than seventy Africans had already died in similar clashes between the two tribes. On January 2, 1960, twenty were killed. This led to the declaration of a state of emergency in mid-January in the province of Kasai. It was the only way the Belgian Col-

onial Government, which was still in power, could deal
with the situation. This step, however, produced no solution.

The Round Table Conference had been in the air for
several weeks and Belgium's attitude to the Congo's future
had altered considerably since Congo leaders first demanded a Brussels meeting with representatives of the Belgian government. The only problem lay in the fact that
political leaders from the Congo had been embittered by
events after the riots (such as imprisonment and subsequent
trials) to such an extent that the Round Table Conference
opened in an emotional and very dangerously charged
atmosphere. This was especially undesirable because cool
thinking and rational ideas were needed in such a meeting,
which was supposed to decide the destiny of the Congo
with her 13,500,000 people. It was, however, most unlikely that the Congo's nationalist leaders would have
agreed to attend the conference in Brussels at this stage
without assurance before hand that general elections were
to be held later, that the installation of an African government would take place within two to three months, and
that full independence would be obtained before the end
of 1960. This situation undoubtedly compelled Brussels
to announce the alteration of the target date of complete
independence from some time in 1964 to June 30, 1960.

The two most prominent African personalities at the
conference were Patrice Lumumba (later elected Prime
Minister of the new Republic) and Joseph Kasavubu
(later elected Chief of State). Mr. Lumumba couldn't
attend the conference until several weeks later as it had
been officially opened in Brussels while he was still in jail.
He had been jailed by the Belgians on political grounds,
although the government stated that he had embezzled

post-office funds. This allegation was seriously doubted because Lumumba's job was far removed from the financial department. Many of his supporters considered his imprisonment as a device to weaken militant opposition to Belgian colonialism, since he had the largest political backing. On January 26, 1960, he was released and flown to Brussels to attend the talks. He arrived in Brussels from Elizabethville with bandaged wrists, telling reporters that on the way to gaol he "was manacled and carried like a log of wood to the plane which took me to Elizabethville. Inside the plane I had my neck twisted. For three days and three nights I was kept manacled and I am covered with wounds." When he was asked whether he thought this was the result of orders to the police by the provincial governor, he replied, "Well, these things happen."[2] But he added that he had been treated well during his three days in the Leotville jail. He was never embittered in the conference because of his previous imprisonment. A quotation from the *Manchester Guardian* of January 28, 1960, page 13 is illustrative:

> Mr. Patrice Lumumba, who was freed from prison to come to the conference and who is emerging as the dominant figure here has been unexpectedly moderate and friendly towards Belgium. He told the conference today that his release could only have meaning if all other political prisoners were also released. "There are today thousands of prisoners and many trials going on in the Congo", he said. "This is unknown to the Belgian people."

Before Mr. Lumumba aired his views about the future of the Congo, the Belgian Minister for the Congo, M. de Schryver, explained to the conference that the June 30,

1960, date for independence had been based on the following timetable:

February 15	Recommendations by the Conference on the Structure of the New State and its electoral system.
February 17	Government appraisal of the recommendations.
March 8	Introduction of the necessary bills in parliament.
March 24	Vote on the bills in parliament.
April 5	Filing of lists of candidates in the Congo for Provincial elections and for the National Chamber of Deputies.
April 15	State of the election campaign.
May 16	Election of the Provincial and National Chamber of Deputies.
June 15	Election of the National Senate.
June 20	Constitution of the Government.
June 30	Meeting of Parliament and the proclamation of independence.

It was after these recommendations by the Minister that Lumumba gave his views on the future of the Congo. "The Belgians are giving us a unified Congo State," he said, "and we should keep it that way instead of breaking it up."[3] He said a central government should be established with a president elected on the United States of America's system of nation-wide suffrage. He explained that this was the only way to stop tribal warfare and inefficient administration. He said that the handling of local affairs would have to be delegated as in the present Belgian system of six provinces but he opposed a federation of Congo states as too weak to deal with problems that would face the new government. It was at this point that Joseph Kasavubu disagreed with Mr. Lumumba and left the conference. He did not like the movement to establish a national state, because this would apparently interfere with his idea of having complete control of the lower Congo region. For this reason it was thought by many Belgians that he was planning to call for the immediate independence of that region. Kasavubu decided to tour some parts of Europe while the conference was going on.

Joseph Kasavubu is known in the Lower Congo as the "King of the Congo." He supports the principle of non-violence of the late Mohandas K. Gandhi, but he is known to be a very poor speaker who reads his French speeches in a halting, squeaky voice as in his own Kikongo language. He is, however, soft-spoken. He was baptized in 1925 and later educated by the Roman Catholic missions who almost made him a priest. It is said that he later became a Protestant. Kasavubu worked as a teacher, an agronomist, a bookkeeper and a civil servant in the colonial administration. But he found his most important role when in 1955 he was elected President of Abako Party, the ethno-cultural association of the Lower Congo, which rapidly became a political machine under Kasavubu's direction. The Abako swept the first municipal elections in Leopoldville in 1957 and got seven out of the eight available burgomasters' seats. Earlier before independence, Kasavubu did not preach separatism. He never showed any tendencies of wanting to go it alone with his Bakongo dreaming of the reconstitution of the seventeenth-century Congo Empire. He tried to convince his followers that they must join forces with nationalists from the Upper

Congo to fight for a federal but not a centralized Congo in which Bakongo autonomy would be guaranteed.

When Kasavubu walked out of the Round Table Conference on January 25, 1960, he lost complete control of his group and later on failed to win back his leadership. Daniel Kanza, vice-president of the Abako, declared that he would recommend to the general assembly of Abako delegates that Mr. Kasavubu be removed as its president. He charged that Kasavubu was leading a campaign in the Lower Congo against the delegates who were continuing to attend the Conference. The Abako delegates explained that Kasavubu had made his statement at the Conference and had walked out without consulting them. Five days later, the Abako cartel of delegates elected Mr. Alphonse Nguvulu, delegate of the People's Party, as the president. This greatly diminished Kasavubu's influence later among his followers. There was even talk later in May whether he would win any seats in the Leopoldville province as a whole. His victory in this area was far from assured. Against the 800,000 Bakongo are half a million Bayaka, most of whom live in the bush-country southeast of Leopoldville. The Bayaka have a common front with the Bapende tribes. Both were aggrieved because of what they say is a Bakongo monopoly on property and jobs in Leopoldville. Against this front and weakened by internal dissension, Kasavubu was said to have only an even chance of securing Leopoldville province. He has no strength at all in the five remaining provinces. Kasavubu is, therefore, strictly a tribal and regional leader who has at times been suspected of plotting the secession of the Lower Congo. Probably the only thing which has discouraged him is the strength of Cleopas Kamitatu, President of Leopoldville province and a Lumumba supporter. We should not, however, underestimate the importance of Kasavubu's Lower Congo. If he succeeds in creating a Bakonko Kingdom it would cut off the rest of the Congo from its only direct access to the sea.

During the Conference the Congolese leaders insisted they must have independence immediately and without any reservations. But several of them expressed themselves in favor of a link between Belgium and the Congo after the latter gained independence. Moise Tshombe, one of the delegates and president of the Conakat Party in Katanga, expressed this view. Dominique Mubanga of the National Progress Party said that Belgium should continue at first to conduct the finances and economic affairs of the new state. This view was opposed by several delegates, the most prominent of them being Paul Bolya, president of the same party. He told the Conference that his group could not sanction any holding back of power but recognized the need for close association between the two states. Other Congolese leaders talked in the same vein inside and outside of the Conference.

Mr. Bolya, who later became a minister in the Lumumba government, is a very striking figure. The author met him in the Congo during the crisis. Bolya has an unusual face, rather like a Congo mask. It is a surprise when it becomes animated. He comes from Equatoria Province. He has a lot of influence, especially among the Mongo, and he has a reputation for honesty. He has managed with great difficulties to weld twenty tribal parties into the PNP. He said, however, that "there is a flicker of tribal feelings. If the other leaders do what the PNP did, we can create a national leadership that can damp down this feeling.

There is no reason why each tribe should not remain what it is, yet agree to co-operate on a national level."[4] Paul Bolya's policy is to blend unitarianism with centralism.

The Round Table talks did not go as smoothly as was expected because of the position taken by the tribal chiefs who wanted to maintain their traditional roles. The chiefs made it clear to the conference that they were dubious about a complete break with Belgium. Some chiefs even denounced those they called "political adventurers" who "claimed" to lead large parties. Several of them said they feared that dictatorship might result when Belgium freed the Congo. One of them, Chief Lwaka Bwanga from Kasai Province, which was then under martial law because of tribal conflict, said that he felt an election would not establish a firm enough control in that region to achieve peace. The chiefs complained further that the press tended to emphasize the views of the political parties, which were centered only in the cities, but ignored the views of tribal leaders who had been conducting rural affairs for many years in concert with the Belgian colonial officials. One of them, Chief Luhina Mwenda-Munongo of Katanga Province, even claimed that of 1,600,000 votes cast in the December, 1959 elections, 1,300,000 came from rural areas, mostly ruled by the chiefs. These allegations were not totally true because most of the political leaders were essentially tribal leaders, deriving their main support from rural areas.

Now a question arises as to the reason why Belgium surrendered its authority so rapidly. Why did she hand the Congo to the nationalists with so little ado? The Belgian government had, of course, made a cold appraisal of the facts. The Congo was no longer subservient and at the same time profitable to Brussels. On the contrary, the

Belgian government argued that it was now a drain on the Belgian taxpayer, who was not unnaturally more interested in his pocket than in the Congo. The Leopoldville riots of January, 1959, were to some extent partly political and tribal clashes, but they were also partly anti-European. These riots and earlier disturbances in different parts of the Congo finally settled the Belgian government's tardy but growing conviction that the Congo was not going to be isolated completely from the flood of African nationalism. Since the final triumph of African nationalism is inevitable, reasoned the Belgian government, let us give the Congo to the Africans now, thus retaining their friendship and avoiding further trouble and expense. At the same time, we can maintain our hold over, and profits from, the great industries, while divesting the drain of administration of the country to the pockets of African taxpayers. What will the future African government do with such sudden power? Will there not be intertribal warfare, with appalling bloodshed, in a local struggle for power—perhaps for many years? We hope not, says Brussels, but if there is, it will not result in Belgians being killed.

It is true that, given a background of educational neglect and administrative discrimination, it may not be in the interest of African good government simply to hand over colonial power whenever an African politician demands it from a public platform. It is also true that some degree of national organization, public experience, and trained personnel is essential to give African states an opportunity to retain any form of cohesion. But it is also true that we can no longer imagine that the colonial powers will do these things easily for us and then hand independence to us on a silver platter without compulsion of some sort.

The idea that some powers continue to hold colonies under "trusteeship" until, in their opinion, the colonies become "capable" of self-government is erroneous and misconceived. No doubt the Congo can teach us many lessons. But surely the most important of them all is that for fifty years the Belgians held the Congo by force, never even knowing—since they permitted no freedom of expression until it was far too late—just how great the hatred was that they had earned. It would seem that the Beligans were guilty not of granting freedom too soon, but of withholding it for too long; of giving only when they were forced to give, and then giving without generosity or grace.

It is therefore, my opinion that if any colonial power in Africa wishes to see an orderly political evolution, they must assert explicitly now that self-government and independence is an early objective. Majority African representation is now an essential and immediate condition if African patience is to be stretched to wait for independence during a reasonable period of progressive training and take-over. The colonial settlers must be told in no uncertain terms that African self-government is coming and that they must come to terms with it. Neglect of this duty must sacrifice the security of the white community itself. Elsewhere, in Southern Rhodesia, South Africa, and the Portuguese territories, continued refusal to recognize that the Africans are destined to govern themselves will only lead to an eventual repetition of the Congo tragedy on a much larger scale.

II

It was quite evident, so far, that only one Congolese leader of national scope had arisen. He was Patrice Lumumba, leader of the Congolese National Movement.

He was strongest in Eastern Province (i.e., Stanleyville or Orientale Province) but had followers all over the Congo. Lumumba was feared and distrusted by Belgians in the Congo. They called him all sorts of names, such as an opportunist who had accepted money from Belgian Communists and they were afraid he would either control a coalition in the new parliament or become a terrorist leader. In any case, Lumumba is a *very popular man* in the Congo, even today.

Before elections which led to independence, Lumumba was considered the most powerful political leader in the Belgian Congo and was hailed by thousands as the messiah of Congolese freedom on an Election Day tour of the African quarters. In an impromptu speech he demanded the immediate abdication of Belgian authority instead of waiting for June 30, the date for independence, but he urged the throng to treat "the white man as a brother." "Don't throw stones at European cars. If you are drinking a glass of African palm wine and a European passes by, please ask him courteously to join you. He is our brother, and we must work together." [5]

There was no denying Lumumba's solid popularity in the left-bank commune of Lubunga. His slow passage though the teeming, rust-colored roads was followed by shrieking mobs waving green boughs and shouting, "*Uhuru*," a Swahili word for Freedom. Arriving back at the ferry landing, Lumumba was engulfed by 3,000 natives who nearly swamped the boat. Climbing to the roof of the boat deck he cried, "The Congo is already the people's Congo." "*Ndio* [Amen]," the throng chorused. Finally after much hooting the ferry boat edged away. In their enthusiasm several adherents of Lumumba leaped fully clothed into the River Congo and swam after it.

There were a lot of accusations that Lumumba had had
some dealings with the Belgian Communists. This he
refuted when he was interviewed in Stanleyville on May
29, 1960. He denied also that he had ever accepted or had
ever been offered money by the Belgian Communist party.
Albert Kalonji, who later declared the secession of Southern
Kasai with Bakwanga as his capital, had a photocopy of
an alleged check for 10,000,000 francs (about $200,000)
that he contended was sent to Lumumba by the Belgian
Communists. He never explained, however, how he got
the photostat copy or who gave it to him. He only
alleged that Lumumba had bought twenty-four Czech
Skoda cars for his party on the strength of the check but
then could not cash it because he did not want to confirm
the transaction revealed by Mr. Kalonji. This accusation
by Kalonji was never verified, so it was dismissed as a
waste of valuable time.

Lumumba continued mapping a program for the country
before the elections. He was not satisfied with the outcome of the Round Table Conference, especially its constitutional arrangements. He, therefore, listed five demands
instead at a press conference in Leopoldville on March 3,
1960. These demands were:

1. Immediate withdrawal of all Belgian troops
   from the Congo.

2. Immediate withdrawal of M. Van der
   Meersch, the Belgian Minister who was sent
   to handle any trouble during the handing
   over of power on June 30, 1960.

3. Election of a Chief of State by direct vote,
   not by a vote of the future National Assembly
   and Upper House sitting as a constituent
   assembly, as now arranged.[6]

4. Scrapping of the design for the national flag—
   a gold star on a blue background with six
   stars down one side representing the six
   provinces which his party claims, bearing the
   taint of colonialism.

5. Appointment of the government leader from
   the party with the largest single majority in
   the elections.

These demands were not met immediately, with the
exception of the last one. This did not please him at all.
But his relationship with Belgium was further strained
when it came to the formation of government just a few
days before independence. The Belgian resident minister,
M. Ganshoj van der Meersch, sent for Patrice Lumumba
as leader of the largest party in parliament and gave him
until 6:30 P.M. on Friday, June 17, to find out if he could
form a government. But two hours before the deadline
expired, he sent for Lumumba, withdrew the mandate and
revealed that he had already invited Joseph Kasavubu,
leader of the Abako tribal party, to form a government
instead. Van der Meersch offered no adequate explanation for this brusque rejection of Lumumba, who had 40
seats in both houses of parliament whereas Kasavubu had
only 12. Lumumba had nearly three times as many. He
was, therefore, convinced that he had been sent for simply
to mislead the public into believing that he had been given
a chance and failed.

Whatever the motive, the maneuver failed. Kasavubu
was obliged to confess to van der Meersch that he did not
have a parliamentary majority, and Lumumba had to be
sent for again. This episode, if it did nothing else, certainly increased Lumumba's dislike of the Belgians, but
not until the morning of June 30 were we permitted to

glimpse the depths of his bitterness and resentment. Independence Day, instead of becoming a day of reconciliation and jubilation, widened the gulf between the Belgians and the Congolese. Lumumba answered King Baudouin's praise of Leopold II with a denunciation of Belgium's colonial record. It was only with difficulty that the King was persuaded to remain for the rest of the day's ceremonies. Lumumba's speech on Independence Day as reported in the *Manchester Guardian* of July 1, 1960, said in part:

> Our wounds are too fresh and too smarting for us to be able to chase them from our memory. We have known ironies, insults, and blows which we had to undergo morning, noon and night because we were Negroes. We have seen our lands spoiled in the name of laws which only recognized the right of the strongest. We have known laws which differed according to whether it dealt with a black man or a white man. We have known the atrocious sufferings of those who were imprisoned for their political opinions or religious beliefs, and of those exiled in their own country. Their fate was truly worse than death itself. Who will forget the rifle-fire from which so many of our brothers perished, or the jails into which were brutally thrown those who did not want to submit to a regime of injustice, oppression and exploitation, which were the means the colonialists employed to dominate us.

Later in the evening Lumumba paid tribute to the King by saying: "At the moment when the Congo reached independence the whole government wishes to pay solemn homage to the King of the Belgians and to the noble people he represents for the work done here over three-quarters of a century. For I would not wish my feelings to be wrongly interpreted."

After the King had left for Brussels, Albert Kalonji, a former Lumumba follower, cabled an apology to King Baudouin for the attack on Belgian colonial rule given June 30, 1960, by the Congolese Prime Minister. The cable said that the Premier's speech was "in no way representative of the feelings of the nation."

Thus the Congo was launched into independence in an atmosphere of suspicion, confusion and recrimination. And scarcely had Lumumba installed himself in the official villa on the banks of the Congo River when Leopoldville was torn by a series of tribal clashes. I shall consider this in detail in the next chapter. It is, however, necessary to analyze the behavior of the Belgian Resident Minister who made such a naive constitutional blunder as calling on Kasavubu, who had the least seats in Parliament, to form a government. Walter G. van der Meersch arrived in the Congo in June at a time when the Congolese and the Belgians were eying each other with mutual distrust and fear. He brought with him the reputation of a strong man, largely derived from his successful prosecution of Belgians who had collaborated with the Nazis during the war. There seems little doubt that the Belgian government, dismayed by the crumbling of Belgian authority and the spreading disloyalty of its citizens in the Congo, had sought a man of unassailable reputation who would win the confidence of Africans and Europeans alike. Mr. van der Meersch was so unsure in his grasp of Congo affairs that when he was interviewed by foreign correspondents all replies were supplied by a secretary. He lacked the knowledge of the African affairs with which he had to deal, and this probably accounts for the mistake he made, thinking that in Africa parliamentary majority does not matter. Still he was a strong man who, as Belgium's Resident Minister, on June 1 took up the task of helping the Congolese to find a Prime Minister. But he greatly deepened Congolese suspicions of Belgian motives.

NOTES: *Chapter 7*

1. *New York Times*, January 4, 1960
2. *The Manchester Guardian*, January 28, 1960, p. 9
3. *New York Times*, January 29, 1960, p. 3
4. Colin Legum, "The Belgian Congo Towards Independence," from *Africa South in Exile*, (London, Africa South Publications, July-Sept. 1960) p. 87
5. *New York Times*, June 16, 1960, p. 4
6. This would have eliminated Kasavubu completely from the political scene because he had no popular backing at all. Lumumba apparently realized this and was desirous of proving to Kasavubu that when confronted with a popular mandate, he could make him (Kasavubu) crawl on his knees.

Part Two

CHAPTER **8**

The Derailment of
the Congo Express

———————————————————————

HISTORY DEMANDS PERSPECTIVE tempered with reality, and in the future the youth of Africa will be able to look back on the events which followed the granting of independence to the Republic of the Congo and see more clearly what significance those events actually carried. To provide an objective account of the Congo crisis should, therefore, be the tasks of those progressive people who have been able to observe the strife in this great African country intimately, especially the Africans. It is an almost impossible task to cover the whole ground of the crisis without letting some facts go, selectively, of course, but my purpose here, nevertheless, is objectivity.

The independence of the Belgian Congo on June 30, 1960 should have brought to an end the long-standing conflict between Africans and Europeans. But this was not the case. Belgian neo-colonialism still lingered on. Generally, colonial powers give political independence to their dependent territories, but retain in one way or another domination of the cultural and economic life of the country. It was clear that the Belgians intended to influence and control the wealthy state of the Congo not only economically and culturally but also politically. The events considered in this chapter show the failures of certain colonial powers to recognize the problems of Africa, and Africa's importance for the international community.

It is difficult to reconstruct all the events that led to the immolation of the freedom of the Congo. Nevertheless, it is possible to trace the events which led to the outbreak of disorder and violence from the middle of June, 1960, when after he had won the elections, Mr. Lumumba was called upon to form a government. It took several days to elect or form a cabinet composed of purely Congolese nationals to take over from the Belgians. Patrice Lumumba with skill and patience tried to knit together all the parties in a coalition government. He even made a deal with the pro-Belgian parties accepting Jean Bolikango as President of the Republic; but when this failed he tried without success to negotiate with Moise Tshombe. Tshombe's demands for cabinet posts to be alloted to his supporters were completely out of proportion to his strength in parliament. Although he emerged from Katanga Province with more seats in the national parliament than, say, Kasavubu, he still did not have as much power as Lumumba had. His demands proved to be too high. In the midst of these tortuous negotiations, the Belgian Minister to the Congo, Walter Ganshof van der Meersch, made a very surprising decision. Without waiting for Lumumba to complete his task of forming a government of national unity, he invited Joseph Kasavubu to take over this responsibility. We should note here that Kasavubu was the only Congolese leader who had refused to negotiate with Lumumba. One can easily understand that it was this action that broke the last tenuous link between Lumumba and the Belgians, for it completely exposed the fact that there was no constitutional legality in the mind of the Belgian Minister. Rather, his actions were dictated chiefly by political expediency. Kasavubu, having very little strength in parliament, was bound to fail miserably, as he did, in even starting negotiations. History will reveal the intentions of the Belgians in their attempt to maneuver things in this way. The Congolese people, who had categorically given their verdict through the ballot box, never knew what went on behind the scenes. When Kasavubu failed to form a government the leaders of the African states, including Dr. Kwame Nkrumah, persuaded the various leaders to co-operate for the sake of African unity and solidarity. They managed to persuade Kasavubu to participate in the negotiations. When parliament met, Lumumba did everything in his power to persuade his followers to vote for Kasavubu in order to achieve Congolese unity and demonstrate Congolese solidarity on matters of national interest. Some supporters of Lumumba tried to warn him against accepting or backing Kasavubu for the presidency, since they had long been rivals, but he completely refused. This showed the readiness of Lumumba to compromise on matters of national interest. Eventually a cabinet was formed with Patrice Lumumba as the first Prime Minister and Joseph Kasavubu as a ceremonial Head of State and Commander in Chief of the Armed Forces. It was on this inauspicious note that the Congo celebrated its independence from June 30 to July 3, 1960. These first four days of independence were declared a national holiday in the whole country, and for the most part they passed in tranquillity. Many cities remained quite calm, and things moved in such a way that nobody seemed to be aware of what was happening. One observer of the scene has vividly described the situation:

> When the great moment of independence came to this nation the surface atmosphere was so calm it

seemed as if most of Leopoldville was unaware of the history being made. The crowds for the various festivities in the inner city were comparatively small and orderly. Cordons of helmeted Congolese troops, still under the command of Belgian officers, were completely in control of all ceremonial areas. Everything, except the hotels and cafes, was shut down. When King Baudouin flew into Leopoldville on the afternoon of June 29 and was driven with top Congolese leaders along the four-lane Albert Boulevard, spectators were relatively few and undemonstrative. In a field just outside Matete there was a scattering of hastily constructed African bush huts, thrown up by "country cousins" of the city tribesmen summoned for the expected fighting. The huts were deserted, and it was the troops' intention to keep them so. As one Congolese official said, "There will be no Belgian paternalism in our suppression of these tribal scraps. The Belgians could not afford to be too harsh for fear everyone would gang up on them. We have no such inhibitions and we have no intention of letting these crazy tribal differences upset our plan."[1]

In other parts of the Congo, such as Elizabethville, the atmosphere was not actually restive, but still one could sense that something was brewing. Minor troubles and incidents were almost bound to occur. Even in April, 1959, the report of the Belgian Parliamentary Commission of Inquiry had stated categorically that individual feelings of vengeance and annoyance among the Congolese were being progressively increased by the European attitude toward black people; that dissatisfaction was rising almost daily. Looking back on that period, now, one can see that it would have been possible to predict that a general uprising would occur. There were clear and unequivocal signs indicating that all was not well in the country. The first indication that the Congolese people had not forgiven the Belgians for their brutal colonial policy was the Prime Minister's independence speech. Many Western writers argue that Mr. Lumumba's speech, delivered before the Belgian King and the assembled dignitaries of the world on June 30, 1960, was ill-conceived. They argue that the extreme tone and contempt in which he spoke condemning Belgian colonialism was rude and unwise, especially when in the presence of Western dignitaries and career diplomats; that he spoke vindictively of the changes that were going to be made. The speech, the argument continues, did nothing to calm what now seems to have been an already restive population; indeed, it is said, it was almost a call to arms and its tone intensely nationalistic. (This speech is fully produced in Appendix A.)

II

With these facts in mind, let us look into the meeting of the Congolese National Army—the Force Publique. As a matter of fact, this is what caused the Congo disaster, and it has been described by various writers in highly emotional and flowery language. Colin Legum writes:

> The disaster when it finally came, came swiftly and from an unexpected quarter. The Congo's hope for a peaceful transition to independence lasted less than a week. On 8 July the Force Publique mutinied in Leopoldville; within three days the riot had spread throughout the Force. But the trouble had already started on 4 July, the day after the independence festivities ended. In ten crucial days the Belgians lost the greater part of their seventy years' work in

the Congo, and the Congolese stood in danger of seeing their freedom torn from their hands. The country was by no means leaderless; but the leaders were at cross-purposes; and powerless. Even the mobs had no real power; their rebelliousness and lust were vindictive and effervescent. They behaved like automata. The pressure of their passion, spent, they lapsed into insensate bullying and truculence, and waited sullenly for the "punishment that never came".[2]

Signs of dissatisfaction by the Congolese National Army began to appear on July 4 when nearly all the official distinguished visitors had packed their bags and left the Congo to settle down to the serious business of developing their new state. Only Dr. Ralph Bunche, who was the official United Nations representative, lingered on to see how things would proceed. When one looks at what happened, it becomes quite clear that it was just as well that he did stay. The Force Publique was not happy about the continuation of Belgian neo-colonialism after independence. No Congolese had been promoted to higher position and the Belgians continued to hold the key positions. When asked about this, they replied that independence was for the civilian population and not for the army. This provoked tremendous indignation among the troops since they had been led to believe that after independence they would be the masters of their own house. This was a sorry indication that the Belgian colonialists and imperialists intended to remain the exploiters of the Congolese people—to put it mildly. Under these circumstances, it should have been quite clear even to the uninitiated that a revolt would occur. Actually, as events showed later, it was not only imminent but had reached the explosive stage. Nevertheless, nobody appears to have paid much attention to the first whiff of trouble which came on July 4. At Camp Hardy—near Thysville, between Leopoldville and the sea—members of the Force Publique, armed with their equipment, menaced their Belgian officers and told them, "We are no longer your monkeys. We are the masters now." The term, "you monkey," was invariably used by the colonialists as a term of abuse and was considered by the Africans as a particularly hateful insult which was bound to create international friction as long as it was used.

When the revolt of the Force Publique occurred, soldiers refused to obey their Belgian officers first at Camp Leopold II and at Camp Hardy in Thysville. They broke open the armory and helped themselves to ammunition. On July 6 there was almost critical anxiety in the Congo. Europeans began to crowd together on a hill in the officers' quarter. The troops demanded, meanwhile, the immediate resignation of General Janssens, the Belgian Commander of the Force Publique who had refused to relinquish his position after independence. They also demanded that the white officers who acted as advisers to the Prime Minister and other Congolese officials be dismissed forthwith. These were to be immediately and speedily replaced by Congolese nationals. While these demands were made, three Belgian soldiers were badly beaten and Prime Minister Lumumba and President Kasavubu came to Thysville to reason with the troops. Although they quickly retrieved the position, it was clear that unless immediate and effective measures were taken to redress the grievances of the troops, further trouble was bound to occur. The Prime Minister and Mr. Anicet Kashamura, who was the Minister of Information in the Lumumba cabinet, attributed the responsibility for the troubles to the Belgian officers and other enemies of

African independence. At this point, the European population was swept by a tremendous wave of panic. Word
began to pour into Belgium about the alleged brutalities
and massacres of the European population by the Congolese National Army. This rumor prompted the Belgian
government to place their military forces on a state of
alert. The Prime Minister, in the meantime, made every
effort, including a speech on the radio, to get the troops
to lay down their arms. He promised their requests would
soon be granted, that they would receive promotions and
increased pay according to their personal competence and
past experience. For a short time the Belgian officers considered the trouble ended; and for the next three days they
carried on as usual. The situation remained extremely
confused in the Lower Congo especially when there were
conflicting reports about the seizure and control of Camp
Hardy in Thysville by the mutineers. It was reported that
the Belgian officers were being badly molested and at the
same time came other reports that this was not true. The
actual case was that the Belgian officers in the army had
regained temporary control over the Force Publique
mutineers. This was demonstrated when no special pre-
cautions were taken by the Belgian officers despite their
allegedly bad plight. Not even the refusal of the Congolese to present themselves for duty from July 7 to July 10
struck their officers as ominous at the time. In my view,
this situation is hard to understand if one credits all the
complaints made subsequently by the Belgians and their
wives from Camp Hardy. It is true that some beatings
took place. A civilian referring to events from July 4 to
July 10 complained that he was badly beaten in Thysville
by the troops who broke into the camp. Another Belgian
complained that he and his wife had been held prisoners

for two days, and that they had been threatened with violence. But it would be unfair to exaggerate the situation as several Belgian officers did during the early part of July. Typical of such exaggerations were those of the Belgian officer from Camp Hardy who said that on July 5 the officers of the Force Publique (by which he meant the Belgian officers) were virtually prisoners, and two of them were stoned and beaten with sticks. I shall not go into detailed descriptions of the reported mishandling of the white women and men by the Conoglese National Army during the mutiny. Nevertheless, there is no doubt that these reports of its violence, whether true or not, whether exaggerated or not, acted as a great poison in the relationship between the new Republic and Belgium—in fact, between white populations and Africans throughout not only Africa but the whole world. Evidence of this contempt for whites could be seen in the welcome which the Africans of other neighboring territories gave to white refugees from the Congo. Most of them were almost naked; in fact their condition was in complete contrast to that of their contemporaries who still enjoyed imposed white domination in places like South Africa, Angola, Mozambique, and the Rhodesias. To me, the plight of Belgian colonialists in the Congo should have been an object lesson to those whites in the above mentioned territories who still insist on perpetuating their economic and political privileges on the ground of such vague and undefined terms as keeping white civilization in Africa, civilizing the natives and improving their economic well-being—while in fact they simply mean the consistent annihilation of the peaceful civilian African population whenever Africans demand their political rights. Witness the genocide carried out by the South African white government under Verwoerd (a man known to have had Nazi leanings during the Second World War); or the Sharpeville massacre of Africans in March, 1959—clear demonstrations to the African people that nothing short of arms will end the policy of apartheid.

The Congo disaster descended upon the population with such speed that the Belgian Minister of Justice, M. Merchvers, reporting on black treatment of the whites on July 28, 1960, said that "acts against the profoundest values of mankind and the civilized concepts of personal integrity have been the rule, as if the word had gone round that both men and women should be humiliated to the greatest possible extent." The Congolese Minister of Information, Anicet Kashamura, did not fully repudiate these statements, but questioned the nature of their exaggeration and hysteria. He pointed out that "after all the Belgians had committed unspeakable acts of extermination on the Congolese people during the rule of Leopold II." It seems, however, that there was no question that the behavior of the Force Publique was atrocious in some respects, whatever might have been their motivations. Reports from other parts of the Congo by the victims of the mutiny were sad. A Belgian woman claimed that on the night of July 5 she was raped sixteen times by Congolese soldiers in her home at Kisantu. Several Belgian civilians were also attacked at Inkisi; and six more women claimed that they were victims of attempted rape. Three Belgians reported that they had been arrested and forced to flatten out rolls of barbed wire with their naked feet. In the Bakongo country, it was reported that white women were forced to cut grass barefoot in the savannah, the only apparent purpose being to humiliate them by forcing them to work as African women worked.

These reports filled the world press with horror. Many

European papers, notably Belgian, gave the impression
that the leaders in the Congo had engendered such a revolt
and supported it fully. Some responsible Belgian cabinet
ministers, however, were more restrained in their language.
The Belgian Prime Minister, M. Eyskens, attributed the
crisis to a few leaders only, with particular reference to
Lumumba, the Prime Minister. But what is often forgotten
is the serious view which the Congolese cabinet took of
what was happening, especially when dissident elements
in the Force Publique stoned a ministerial car on July 7.
As has been stated, the mutiny was aimed mainly at Belgian officers in the army and strong resentment was expressed by the army against Lumumba's decision to ap-
point Belgians to national defense posts. However, when
the army met to discuss their grievances at Camp Leopold
II, some officers who tried to break up the meeting were
disobeyed and disarmed. This offered some hope. In fact,
Lumumba at this time spoke very confidently of the future
of the Congo, although he was aware trouble had begun.
He tried his best, together with Kasavubu, to calm the
white population and instill confidence in them, but developments in other parts of the Congo almost overwhelmed them. Eventually, the Congolese cabinet, hoping
to break the tension, agreed to the removal of the Belgian
Commander of the Force Publique, Lieutenant General
Emile Janssens, and his staff. They also agreed that all
Congolese noncommissioned officers should be promoted
one rank. Although this proposal failed to achieve its purpose, it was a step in the right direction.

As a result of these developments, the Belgian Ambassador in Leopoldville advised his government to dispatch
troops to the Congo. This was done against the advice of
other foreign diplomats in Leopoldville, since the situation

had not deteriorated so far as to warrant such a step. It would also constitute a violation of the Congo's territorial integrity and independence. Moreover, the troops from Brussels poured into Leopoldville, which was comparatively calm by now, while the real trouble was at Thysville, approximately eighty-five miles away from Leopoldville. On July 11 the Belgian paratroops occupied Leopoldville and dispersed to all parts of the country. Their arrival was the signal for the rebellion to flare up everywhere in the country. The simmering discontent erupted in previously calm parts of the Congo. There was a riot in the Belgian military base at Matado and Kamina. The same thing happened in Stanleyville, the capital of Orientale Province. The troops in Kengola Camp in Katanga also mutinied, and on the same day they overwhelmed and disarmed Belgian officers in the General Gulliard Camp in Luluabourg, the capital of Kasai Province. It was also on July 11 that Moise Tshombe chose to declare unilaterally the independence of Katanga Province. The fact that his decision coincided with the influx of the Belgian Army, broke the camel's back. It was difficult to avoid the impression that the Congo was being taken over by the Belgians and their allies. From then on the tide of violence rose sharply, and the situation deteriorated swiftly. Grievances fastened on rumors, rumors fed suspicions, and suspicions fanned the forces of mutiny and rebellion.

Before considering the appeal to the United Nations by Lumumba to send troops to oust the Belgians, I would like to review the effects of the revolt. In the first instance, the mutiny of the Force Publique unearthed Belgian maneuvers for political and economic dominance over the Congo even after independence. The monster of neocolonialism was rearing its ugly head again. Secondly, the mutiny completely shattered, for the time being anyway, any spirit of co-operation that might have existed between the Congolese people and the Belgians. Colin Legum writes:

> The mutiny changed everything; it destroyed what was hopeful in the situation; it killed cooperation between the Belgians and the Congolese; it splintered the brittle alliances of the Coalition Government; it opened the way for foreign intervention; and it wrecked internal security. Those trained to uphold law and order were themselves the leaders of lawlessness and disorder. Here was the final irony: the instrument, fashioned by the Belgians at the outset of their occupation of the Congo to establish and maintain their rule turned in their hands to destroy them. Nobody had foreseen this possibility. On the eve of the mutiny, the Commander of the Force Publique, General Janssens, attended an American July 4 party in Leopoldville. Laughing and joking, he met questions about the security position in the Congo with easy confidence: "The Force Publique? it is my creation. It is absolutely loyal. I have made my dispositions." Three days later he was dismissed; a few days more and Force Publique had become the rogue elephant of the Congo.[3]

From that moment the story took a different turn. Prime Minister Lumumba seeing the seriousness of the situation appealed to the United States of America for military assistance to repel the Belgian aggressor. Since this would create political and military complications for the North Atlantic Treaty Organization of which Belgium is a member, the United States' refusal to grant Lumumba's request must have been expected. And, on July 12, the White House press secretary, James Hagerty, announced that

President Eisenhower and Secretary of State Christian H. Herter had denied the Congo's request for American troops. The explanation was given that it would be better for the Congo if troops were to be sent there from the United Nations and not from any of the large Western powers. At that time the Conference of Independent African States, with the initiative of the Osagyefo, Dr. Kwame Nkrumah of Ghana, advised Lumumba to request international assistance directly from the United Nations. This decision was made by Lumumba on July 12, and the story took a new turn.

History will find it hard to understand how the United Nations—called in by the central government of Premier Patrice Lumumba to assist, according to its July, 1960 resolution, that government to secure the complete withdrawal of Belgian forces and to protect the Congo's sovereignty and integrity—paved the way to the overthrow of that government, the dissolution of the parliament which had elected that government, the murder in cold blood of that government's Prime Minister by a Belgian officer (one of those whom the United Nations was to have expelled from the Congo), and the tearing apart of the living body of the Congo Republic. Perhaps it can be explained in terms of one of the greatest problems of the twentieth century: the conflict between a powerful and increasingly strong nationalism and a still living but weakening and desperate imperialism. It is a conflict which in the very deepest sense concerns the moral stature of mankind. Almost without exception, every conflict in today's world is between some type of imperialism and some type of nationalism. Indeed, imperialism and, what is worse, the imposition of its power to force the continued division of national territory, is the fundamental cause of almost all international tensions and threats to peace in contemporary times. The secession of the province of Katanga engineered by Belgium is a case in point. The President of the Republic of Indonesia, Mr. Sukarno, has said that there can be coexistence in the world between the capitalistic and communistic systems. But there can never be coexistence between the forces of imperialism and the forces of nationalism.

In any case, the mutiny of the Force Publique, the intervention by the Belgian troops sent from Belgium, and the failure to maintain a smooth and well-functioning administration, all combined to derail the Congo express. To put it back onto the track, the Congo appealed to the United Nations for military assistance.

NOTES: *Chapter 8*

1. Jack Mendelsohn, Jr., "Uhuru Comes to the Congo," *Africa Today*, VII, (September, 1960) pp. 6-7
2. Colin Legum, *Congo Disaster, op. cit.,* p. 106
3. Colin Legum, *Ibid*, pp. 110-111

CHAPTER 9

The United Nations Action

No EVENTS IN AFRICA'S MODERN HISTORY have been more significant than those which have shaken the Congo since the middle of 1960. Here has been the supreme testing ground of the struggle for Africa's liberation. Congo is the continent's linchpin, Africa's great mineral heart and politico-strategic gateway. All sorts of minerals like uranium, cobalt, copper, diamonds, gold, zinc, manganese, cadmium, columbium, and tantaleum lie buried in its soil in measureless quantities. To the northeast of this huge rich territory lies the Sudan and the route to the United Arab Republic; to the north and northwest, the weak young states of the French community which call themselves the Brazzaville powers; to the southwest, the smoldering furnace of Angola; to the east, we have the huge East African territories of Uganda and Tanganyika, and beyond we can see Kenya, with its rapid advance toward complete independence; southward the way is open to the rich copper belt of Northern Rhodesia and down through Southern Rhodesia to the final bastion of white domination, the Union of South Africa.

The importance of the Congo can therefore hardly be ignored—a quick look at the African map will immediately reveal this. Dr. Kwame Nkrumah has repeatedly said that the Congo, being the heart of Africa, cannot be permitted to become a center of colonial and imperial aggressions in which puppet regimes will be planted. A commentator like Jack Woddis, in his *Africa—The Lion Awakes*, writes that "genuine independence for the Congo would mean more than the loss of the immense mineral wealth owned by Belgian, American, British, French and West German monopolies; more than the deprivation to the West of vital strategic raw materials—cobalt and uranium. Politically it would open the way to the liberation from colonialism of all the remaining territories of Africa which are yet to win their independence. It is, in fact, precisely in those territories lying east and south of the Congo that some of Africa's greatest battles are yet to come."

It is understandable, therefore, that it has been the Congo which has witnessed the first major push and trial of the new imperialist method of neocolonialism. Those peoples in Africa and Asia who have been for a long time subjected to colonialism and imperialism could not help suspecting the intentions of the Western powers in the Congo debacle. The Congo was to be granted formal independence while the colonial advisers remained the real power behind the throne and thus insured that the exploitation of the Congo's riches and manpower by Western monopolies would continue undisturbed.

In the meantime, in New York, members of the Security Council unanimously recommended to the General Assembly that the Republic of the Congo (Leopoldville) should be admitted to membership in the United Nations. A cable dated July 1 from the Prime Minister of the Republic of the Congo, Patrice Lumumba, to the Secretary General, Dag Hammarskjöld, had requested admission to membership in the United Nations. He declared that the Republic of the Congo accepted without reservation the obligations stipulated in the United Nations Charter and would abide by them in absolute loyalty and good faith. Tunisia and Belgium supported the application. During the discussions in the Security Council several members were quite aware and concerned about the Congo's future. Some representatives said that the new Republic had an exceedingly difficult task ahead of it and expressed the hope that it would be able to develop in order and peace, and they assured it that it could count on the assistance of the United Nations and of its members. The Secretary General's wise initiative in sending Mr. Ralph Bunche to be present at the proclamation of independence of the Congo and to study the situation with a view to enabling the United Nations to provide all possible assistance to the young African state, was widely acclaimed.

As we have seen, the Congo was gripped by confusion, fear, and disorder as the result of a vicious circle of events following her accession to independence. Mutinies of the Force Publique, outbursts of violence against Europeans, the sending of metropolitan Belgian troops to protect and evacuate the threatened Europeans, and the mass departure of large numbers of these Europeans resulted in the collapse of many public services and important economic enterprises. It was the sending of the Belgian troops to the Congo that occasioned the request sent to the United Nations Secretary General on July 12 by the President and the Prime Minister of the Congo for the urgent dispatch of military assistance to protect the national territory of the Congo against external aggression (a threat to international peace and security).

The main complaint by the two Congolese leaders was that by dispatching unilaterally her metropolitan troops to the Congo, Belgium had flagrantly violated the treaty of friendship signed between them on June 29, 1960, under the terms of which Belgian troops could intervene only on the express request of the Congolese government, and no such request had been made. They regarded the Belgian action as an act of aggression, therefore, and accused Belgium of having fostered a colonialist conspiracy by carefully preparing the secession of Katanga with a view to maintaining a hold on the Congo. The two leaders also made it quite clear in a telegram of July 13 to the Secretary General that the purpose of the military aid they requested was not to restore the internal situation in the Congo but to protect the national territory against acts of aggression posed by the presence of Belgian troops. They also stated that the request related only to a United Nations force consisting of military personnel of neutral countries and not of the United States, and that if such aid were not forthcoming, the Congo would be compelled to appeal to the Banding Treaty Powers. The aid was requested by the Congo in the exercise of its sovereign rights over its territory.

The Security Council met urgently on the evening of July 13 in response to a request by Secretary General Dag Hammarskjöld, to hear a report by him on a request for United Nations military assistance to the Republic of the Congo. According to Article 99 of the Charter, the "Secretary General may bring to the attention of the Security Council any matter which in his opinion may threaten international peace and security." The Secretary General considered that the matter which he was bringing to the Security Council's attention might threaten the maintenance of international peace and security. This meeting continued for seven hours—until nearly 3:30 A.M. on July

14. After debate in which Soviet proposals to condemn Belgium's action as "armed aggression" and to call for the "immediate" withdrawal of its troops as well as restricting the proposed military assistance to that "made available by African member states of the United Nations," were all rejected, a resolution was finally passed. It authorized the Secretary General, in consultation with the Congolese government, to arrange for the military assistance which would be necessary until the Congolese forces, through the efforts of the Congolese government with the technical assistance of the U.N., could fully meet their tasks. The Council also called on Belgium to withdraw its troops. The Security Council Resolution in full stated:

> Considering the report of the Secretary General on a request for United Nations action in relation to the Republic of the Congo.
>
> Considering the request for military assistance addressed to the Secretary General by the President and the Prime Minister of the Republic of the Congo, (document S/4382),
>
> One: Calls upon the Government of Belgium to withdraw their troops from the territory of the Republic of the Congo.
>
> Two: Decides to authorize the Secretary General to take the necessary steps, in consultation with the government of the Republic of the Congo, to provide the Government with such military assistance, as may be necessary, until, through the efforts of the Congolese Government with the technical assistance of the United Nations, the national security forces may be able, in the opinion of the Government, to meet fully their tasks;

Three: Requests the Secretary General to report to the Security Council as appropriate.

The Resolution was adopted by 8 votes in favor, i.e., Argentina, Ceylon, Ecuador, Italy, Poland, Tunisia, Russia, and the United States of America; and 3 abstentions, i.e., China, France, and the United Kingdom. There were no members opposed. This was in accordance with the Secretary General's request for the Council's speedy action, since the presence in the Congo of Belgian troops, which the Belgian Government said were there to protect human life and to maintain law and order, could not be accepted as a satisfactory stopgap arrangement pending the restoration of order through a national security force. On the contrary, he said, the presence of those troops was a source of internal, and potentially also of international, tension. He also considered that the arrangement envisaged by the Congo Government, i.e., technical assistance of a military nature, was preferable to any other formula. He added that it would be understood that, were the United Nations to act as proposed, the Belgian government would see its way to a withdrawal.

The logic of the Secretary General's argument is reinforced by Charter provisions, which state that all member states expected to "develop friendly relations among them on respect for the principle of equal rights and self-determination of peoples, and to take other appropriate measures to strengthen universal peace." Moreover, the Charter further states that the "Organization is based on the principle of the Sovereign equality of all its members, and all members shall refrain in their international relations from the threat or use of force against the territorial integrity and political independence of any state, or in any other manner

inconsistent with the purposes of the United Nations."
The Belgian government committed an unprecedented
violation of the U.N. Charter by sending her troops to
another sovereign and completely independent territory
(under the pretext of preserving law and order). It was no
business of the Belgian government to restore law and
order in the Congo without the express request from the
Congolese government according to the Treaty of Friendship signed between the two countries on June 29, 1960.

II

Nothing could be more explicit than the Security Council resolution of July 14, 1960. And yet the idea has been
spread far and wide (to, among others, the opponents of
colonialism) that the United Nations was called in "to
restore law and order." These words never appeared in the
resolution, which did not deal with internal Congolese
matters but with the aggression by the Belgians and the
assistance to be given to the Congolese government to
overcome this attack. The interpretation of the Security
Council resolution, therefore, became a matter of great
concern to the African people. It became a point of departure and a source of suspicion in the Congolese affair.
The Secretary General insisted in his first report on the
implementation of the Security Council Resolution S/4387
of July 14, 1960, that since the said resolution was adopted
in response to his initial statement to the Council, the initial statement might, therefore, be regarded as the basic
document in the interpretation of the mandate. He made
clear his view of the main purpose of the introduction of a
United Nations Force in the Congo as well as of the relationship between this action and a withdrawal of Belgian troops.

The general terms with regard to what legal principles should apply to the operation were also stated in the Secretary General's presentation to the Security Council. It was vital at this time that the re-establishment of the instruments of the Government for the maintenance of order should be undertaken immediately if a sound and lasting solution to the difficulties which had arisen in the Congo were to be overcome. The Secretary General implied that it was the breakdown of those instruments which had created the situation leading to the Congo's request for United Nations intervention. Thus, the two main elements from the legal point of view were, on the one side, the Congo's request and, on the other hand, the implied finding that the temporary security force was to be supplied by the United Nations in order to assist the Congolese government to re-establish its administration, specifically in the field of security.

We have just outlined the legal grounds for the U.N.'s entry into the Congo. Once there, how did the U.N. interpret its role in this crisis? The Secretary General argued that, although the United Nations Force was dispatched to the Congo at the request of the government and would be present in the Congo with its consent, and although it might be considered as serving as an arm of the government for the maintenance of order and protection of life (tasks which naturally belong to the national authorities and will pass to such authorities as soon as, in the view of the government, they are sufficiently firmly established), the Force was necessarily under the exclusive command of the United Nations, vested in the Secretary General under the control of the Security Council. This, the Secretary General explained, was in accordance with the principles generally applied by the organization. It was, therefore, interpreted that the Force was thus not under the orders of the government nor could it be permitted to become a party to any internal conflict. It was believed that a departure from this principle would seriously endanger the impartiality of the United Nations and of the operation.

If this interpretation had been strictly adhered to, the Congo could have been saved much misery. Under the prevailing conditions in Africa, this interpretation was unrealistic. It was impossible to be "impartial," and the United Nations was bound to make grievous mistakes. Instead of assisting the legal central government which had called it in, it secured the downfall of that government. Paying the Force Publique when Mobutu was in command but not when General Victor Lundula was in command, although such a request had been submitted by Lundula, gave the clear impression that the Organization was backing the rebels and hoisting them into office. When it was a question of stopping Mobutu from closing down Parliament or saving the lives of the legal Prime Minister, Lumumba, and his colleagues, the U.N. claimed that it had no authority to intervene. Yet it did not hesitate to intervene when it was a question of preventing the Congolese Premier from using his own radio to broadcast to his people. It acted promptly to deny the Lumumba government access to its own airfields, but allowed those same airfields to be used by the Belgians and Tshombe to drag the beaten, bloodied body of Lumumba from Leopoldville to Katanga and death. However, there is no space or intention here to narrate all the sordid details of the betrayal of the Congo. The big question for Africa and the world is why did this happen? Why was it possible for this terrible series of events to take place?

III

The responsibility for the Congo disaster rests first and foremost with the Belgians and their Western allies. No one really believes that a small country like Belgium could have defied the might and economic power of the United States and other Western countries. Only the backing of other countries friendly to Belgium could have produced the present disaster in the Congo. There is no doubt in anybody's mind that Mobutu, Tshombe, Kasavubu, and their accomplices were the tools of foreign interests in the Congo.

Secondly, French imperialism, with its huge financial stakes in Katanga, plotted against the legal government from its hide-out across the river in Brazzaville, hoping to pull off a deal through its puppet Abbe Youlou, President of the Congo Republic (Brazzaville). The visits which were exchanged between Tshombe and Youlou were a clear demonstration of what was happening. The French were ready to send in French military aircraft and other forms of assistance to help oust the legal government.

Thirdly, the Soviet Union, looking for a toe hold in the Congo, rushed eagerly to make its aid available to the legal government headed by Patrice Lumumba. With the West turned against him, including the United Nations which was supposed to help him restore law and order, Lumumba was put in the situation of having no option but to accept Soviet aid. The United Nations refused not only to co-operate in his attempts to bring back Katanga into the central government but also thwarted Lumumba's action by seizing the radio station and the airports. This was, of course, a violation of the Secretary General's interpretation of the neutrality of the Force, which interpretation was in itself a source of great doubt and dispute. It was the Soviet Union that offered to assist the central government to restore law and order in the whole Republic. The Belgians had just opened a bank for Tshombe in Katanga in the month of August, thereby solidifying and consolidating Katanga's claim to secede. The United Nations did not even protest this flagrant Belgian interference in the internal affairs of the Republic of the Congo. In other words, in the early phase of the crisis the U.N. appeared to have adopted an ambivalent attitude toward Belgium's open interference in Congolese affairs under the pretext of being neutral. The German Federal Republic was also eager to have a foothold in the Congo, and so made their airports available. The United Kingdom with its big monopoly, the Tanganyika Concessions, which had shares in the Union Minière, was not indifferent to which way the wind of change would blow. Not only has the Tanganyika Concessions shares in the Union Minière, but the Belgians have shares in the Tanganyika Concessions. And the Americans have shares in both. British interests in Rhodesia were interested too. And the British shareholders in the Benguela railway, with its links from Katanga to Angola, and to the copper belt and down to Wankie coal mines, were also interested. These people all had their eyes on the situation. Recruitment officers for Tshombe were set up in numerous European capitals. Recruitment agents went to work in Salisbury, Johannesburg, and Nairobi. The combined forces of the imperialist powers were, in fact, thrown against the Congo.

The principle which evolved for guidance of the U.N. Force in the Congo was that, while on its side the host government when exercising its sovereign right over the

Force should be guided by good faith in the interpretation
of the purpose of the Force, the United Nations, on its
side, should also be understood to be determined by similar
good faith in its interpretation of the maintenance of the
Force in the host country. This was to be the basic understanding regarding the presence of a United Nations Force
in the Congo. This meant that the U.N. should have freedom of movement within its area of operations, free access
to that area, and all facilities necessary for a successful
accomplishment of the task. It should be noted that for
specification of what was to be considered the area of
operations, agreement with the central government was
required.

There is no doubt that the central government accepted
these interpretations. Moreover, many people in the Congo
and in Africa regard the United Nations as an impartial,
neutral, above-conflict adjudicator, as a referee, the voice
and conscience of the world, a protector of the weak and
oppressed, a dispenser of justice. Its presence in the Congo
was, therefore, greatly welcomed. But this idealist conception of the U.N. is divorced from reality, from the
actual world in which we live. The organization as a body
represents the imperialist states, other smaller capitalist
countries, the newly independent states of Africa and Asia,
the countries of Latin America, and the people of the socialist or communist camp (though still excluding Communist China). This necessarily implies that the United
Nations is by no means united in its deliberations even
when facing a crisis such as the Congo. It represents a real
world, and mirrors the conflicts of that world. Each vital
policy decision, therefore, becomes a battle of contending
interests, between those who stand for peace and genuine
independence for nations, and those who do not. Some of

them regard the underdeveloped areas of the world as sources of profit and as strategic bases. It is, therefore, difficult to carry out a decision even if, after discussion and concession, some agreement has been reached on paper. With regard to this point Jack Woddis writes:

> This is where the major problem really lies. For even when the U.N. Security Council adopts such a correct and progressive resolution as the resolution of 14 July 1960, the machinery for implementing it, though it is often referred to as "an international civil service", is not controlled by the United Nations but by only one side of this body. The machinery of the U.N., the U.N. "state apparatus" as it were, is mainly in the hands of the Western powers, and their supporters. Just consider these facts: Of 28 deputies to the Secretary-General, 17 are from the United States or its allies, 10 from neutral or former colonial countries, 1 from the Socialist countries. Out of 34 directors, 28 are from the first named group, 5 from the second, and 1 from the third. Since 1955, some 2,000 technical experts from America and its allies have been sent to various countries by the U.N.; none has been sent from Africa, and only 40 from the Socialist countries.[1]

Although improvements are being made in the Operational and Executive Personnel Program of the U.N., it has been the general experience in U.N. appointments of many kinds that the chief criterion in the selection of these officers should be personal competence, while in the establishment of organs of limited membership the main requirements should be that the members are sufficiently expert to fulfill the tasks assigned to them and sufficiently representative to enjoy the greatest possible degree of confidence of the whole. The more heterogeneous the membership of any international body, the more the criterion of personal competence in the selection of officers tends to give way to some principle of rotation or equitable distribution.

Commenting on the U.N. Congo operation, Woddis writes: "And for the U.N. Congo operation, 45 military staff officers from America and its allies, none from the Socialist countries; 546 representatives in police and liaison units in the Congo from the Western powers, 24 from Africa, and none from the Socialist countries; 220 nonmilitary staff from the Western powers, none from the Socialist countries. So much for the oft-vaunted impartiality of the U.N. apparatus." [2]

The main point here is that the United Nations Secretariat and its bodies are so overloaded with Western representatives, particularly susceptible to pressure from the United States as the most influential power, that it is inevitable that the United Nations apparatus is neither equipped in personnel nor politically disposed to carry through any just resolutions of the United Nations, but would constantly seek to stall on them or to ignore them completely and do the opposite to what the resolutions demand. I would not, however, go so far as to say that the United Nations apparatus was in the hands of the enemies of the Congolese people. But it would appear that certain powerful interests made possible the setting at nought of the Security Council Resolution of 14 July, 1960.

Before the Secretary General embarked on the fulfillment of the Security Council Resolution, he made clear his idea about the composition of the United Nations Force in the light of previous experience. In the U.N. report (document A/3943), it was stated that "while the United Nations must reserve for itself the authority to decide on the composition of such [military] elements, it is obvious that the host country, in giving its consent, cannot be indifferent to the composition of those elements." The report continues: "In order to limit the scope of possible differences of opinion, the United Nations in recent operations has followed two principles: Not to include units from any of the permanent members of the Security Council; and not to include units from any country which, because of its geographical position or for other reasons, might be considered as possibly having a special interest in the situation which has called for the operation." It would seem desirable to accept such a formula because, while it is for the U.N. alone to decide on the composition of military elements sent to a country, the U.N. should, in deciding on the composition, take fully into account the viewpoint of the host government as one of the most serious factors in guiding the recruitment of the personnel. Usually this means that serious objections by the host country against participation by a specific contributing country in the U.N. operation will determine the U.N.'s decision. In the case of the Congo crisis, assistance was to be sought, in the first place, from African nations. Military units in the U.N. Congo Force from any of the permanent members of the Security Council were to be excluded automatically. But it became quite clear during the latter part of the crisis that this principle was violated in one way or another by the great powers. The government of the Soviet Socialist Republics decided to send supplies to the legal government of the Congo headed by Patrice Lumumba. Other powers, who were determined to oust Lumumba, sent supplies to various groups.

It was reported in the *Manchester Guardian* of July 20,

1960, that twenty American servicemen had been sent to Leopoldville by the State Department. Russia immediately protested to the United States against the reported arrival of these servicemen. Mr. Gromyko, the Soviet Foreign Minister, handed a statement to the American envoy in Moscow saying that the "Soviet Government considers it necessary to draw the attention of the Government of the United States to the fact that the sending of the above-mentioned American military group into the capital of the Republic of the Congo is an impermissible act. In this connection, the Soviet Government protests to the United States of America and expects the above-mentioned military group to be withdrawn from the territory of the Republic of the Congo at once." Mr. Gromyko stated further that the Soviet government deemed it necessary to mention likewise that unless the above-mentioned group of American soldiers and officers was withdrawn, the Soviet Government would have to draw due conclusions from this for its actions. Apparently, the American government did not deny these allegations, but, according to the State Department spokesman, Mr. Lincoln White, the Soviet Union was only trying to befog the issue and to put the worst possible light she could upon a so-called highly effective and co-operative effort on the part of many countries with the United Nations to lend assistance to the Congo government and its people. On July 24, a newspaper in Paris (*Le Monde*) said: "In reality Russia is engaging today in a vast political operation. To present the Congolese tragedy as one of the elements of a general plot by American and even German imperialism, though the U.S. has refused to send troops even within the framework of the United Nations, is to mount, for evident propaganda ends, a shameful fable."

Actually, there was tremendous confusion here. The fact

is that, whatever the various governments said in their cold-war spirit and language, they did not fully co-operate with the U.N. A statement by the U.S. Defense Department spokesman admitted that America had sent about 100 servicemen to the Leopoldville area and there were about twenty Army men assigned to the U.S. Embassy in Leopoldville to assist in evacuation work (they were using helicopters and light aircraft for the task). In addition, there were about eighty Air Force men at Leopoldville (Ndjili) Airport in connection with the U.N. airlift. One would be entitled to ask why this was necessary since the United Nations had been assigned the task of insuring complete order and security in the whole country, and no state, especially those which are members of NATO, was supposed to send any troops to the Congo. The American Defense Department spokesman said that all U.S. troops in the Congo were engaged in carrying out humanitarian work of the U.N. He added: "We have no combat troops there and no intention of sending any." (See *Manchester Guardian* of July 20, 1960). The Security Council resolution was clear enough to render this argument inadequate. Moreover, the Belgians had given the "humanitarian reason" of service in the Congo as a pretext while they carried out acts of aggression against the Congolese state.

The Soviet government also decided at this time to send some of her people to the Congo. This complicated the Congo scene. The West became completely panicked and hysteria swept the U.N. corridors. The cold war had crept into the Congo in reality now. The question of Congolese independence and integrity became a secondary matter. The struggle assumed international proportions, with the West working frantically to stem a Communist take-over and the Socialists doing likewise. However, there were actually few people from the Socialist countries in the

Congo at that time. I saw only about ten in Leopoldville whereas people from America, France, Belgium, U.K., West Germany, and some neutral countries were innumerable. It appeared to me that there was a deliberate attempt to thwart the efforts of the legal prime minister, and even to dismember the new country. I do not completely ignore the co-operative attitude adopted by various governments. For instance, the official Soviet news agency, Tass, reported that Russia was prepared to place five airliners at the disposal of the Ghana government for transporting Ghanaian troops to the Congo. As a result of this announcement, three IL-18 aircraft left Moscow the morning of July 19 for Leopoldville with food supplies for the Congo, and were to be directed to Accra after delivering their supplies. More than 10,000 tons of wheat and other foodstuffs were taken to the Congo shortly afterward by the Soviet freighter *Leninogorsk*. Nevertheless, there were clear evidences of desperate and almost frantic efforts by certain countries to obstruct the constructive work being done by the U.N. in the Congo. The tragedy was that no protest was launched by the Secretary General and, instead, people remained almost silent whenever Belgian interfered with the work of the Organization in one way or another.

To come back to the composition of the U.N. Force in the Congo and its essential principles, on July 14 the Secretary General appointed Major General C. Carlsson von Horn of Sweden as Supreme Commander of the U.N. Force to be sent to the Congo. General von Horn had been Chief of Staff of the U.N. Truce Supervision Organization in the Middle East (UNTSO) since March, 1958. He was to be assisted by eleven military officers, eight Field Service men and five radio officers who were to be drawn from the UNTSO headquarters in Jerusalem.

On July 15 the first troops of the U.N. Force from

Ghana and Tunisia arrived in the Congo. By the end of the day, 600 had been air-lifted to Leopoldville, and other troops in Morocco, Ethiopia, Tunisia, and Ghana were ready for departure. The United States and the United Kingdom pledged contributions of food to be air-lifted to the Republic. Six military advisers from Canada, Denmark, Italy, New Zealand, Norway, and Sweden were also en route to the Congo. Henry R. Labouissie, former director of the United Nations Relief and Works Agency for Palestine Refugees in the Near East, was asked to assist the Secretary General in setting up the U.N. Force. At the same time, Mr. Hammarskjöld named Dr. Sture C. Linner, a Swedish businessman, as resident representative of the Technical Assistance Board in the Republic of the Congo. A group of U.N. Secretariat members left New York to serve the U.N. mission in the Congo and Dr. Ralph Bunche was appointed Commander of the U.N. Force pending the arrival of General von Horn. All this was indicative of the positive attitude of co-operation adopted by the various peoples, organizations, and governments in the face of the crisis. The government of India informed the Secretary General that it would supply 1,000 tons of wheat for the Congo, while contingents for the United Nations Force continued to pour in from Tunisia, Ghana, Morocco, and Ethiopia and were deployed by Dr. Bunche, the Commander *ad interim*. On July 18, plans were announced for the Swedish battalion with UNEF to move to the Congo; while 635 men were to be air-lifted to Leopoldville on July 20 for one month. By July 18, more than 4,000 troops in seven battalions from five African countries had been accepted. Of that number, 3,500 had arrived in the Congo (460 from Ethiopia, 770 from Ghana, 1,250 from Moscow, 1,020 from Tunisia); and 700 from Guinea were to be air-lifted later in the week. In addition, an offer from the Mali Federation had been accepted, for activation later. While the military build-up was going on, individual experts on various fields were also being appointed. The Secretary General invited Brigadier I. J. Rikhye of India, former Chief of Staff of the United Nations Emergency Force, to serve as his military advisor at the U.N. head-quarters. Maurice Pate, Executive Director of the U.N. Children's Fund, left for the Congo to advise on the proc-essing, transport, and distribution of food during the food emergency. Thus, the first phase of building of the U.N. Force had been completed with acceptance of the above-mentioned African units. But for the second phase the Secretary General sought troops from three European, one Asian and one Latin-American country. On request, Swe-den had given permission for the transfer of 635 men from its contingent with the U.N. Emergency Force in Gaza to the Congo. The admixture of the U.N. Force in the Congo in which African troops were to serve side by side with European, Asian, and Latin-American troops was explicitly explained by Mr. Hammarskjöld in his first report to the Security Council on the implementation of its resolu-tion S/4387 of July 14, 1960. Speaking on the composition of the Force, he said:

> The ultimate solution to the problem that has given rise in the Congo has to be found by the Republic of the Congo itself, with the assistance of the United Nations. In the same spirit I believe that, to the ex-tent that the Republic of the Congo needs interna-tional assistance, such assistance should, within the framework of the United Nations, in the first instance be given by its sister African nations, as an act of African solidarity. However, this natural reliance

on regional solidarity for the solution of a problem of this kind should be qualified by an element of universality, natural—and indeed essential—to any United Nations operation. Therefore, while the Force, in my view, should be built around a hard core of military units from African states, it should also, to the extent which might be found practical, include units from other areas which meet the general conditions for the composition of a United Nations Force to which I have referred above.[3]

Thus, Mr. Hammarskjöld viewed the operation as a manifestation of the willingness and ability of the African states to help within the framework of the United Nations. Help from other regions which were included in the Force was to be considered as assistance given, in the spirit of the Charter, to the African community of nations. With this approach, the operation in the Congo should have served to strengthen also the ties of these countries within the United Nations and with the world community. "It would be wholly unjustified to interpret the United Nations action in the sense that nations from outside the region step into the Congo situation, using the United Nations as their instrumentality, because of the incapability of the Congo and of the African states themselves to make the basic contribution to the solution of the problem," the Secretary General said. It was clear that Mr. Hammarskjöld was mainly guided by this interpretation of the United Nations operation in his efforts to build up the Force. For that reason, he addressed himself first to African states for troops, appealing in a second stage to other nations which met the conditions that were generally applicable. At the same time, he continued his efforts to activate further African units to the extent necessary. Further, he addressed a series of appeals for support in such fields as logistics, signals, material, aircraft, and specialized personnel to those countries which were most likely to provide them at very short notice, irrespective of their geographical position. Apart from being influenced by the above factors, the Secretary General was guided by considerations of availability of troops, language, and geographical distribution within the region.

The rapid action taken by the U.N. authorities in building up the Force and its consequent dispatch to Leopold-ville had already had a salutary effect by July 18, and the growing recognition of its role as a Force for the restoration of peace and order was bound to contribute to its increasing effectiveness. The African states played their role wonderfully well. They demonstrated their realization that to grow into independence means to grow into interdependence. But to grow into interdependence means also to assume international responsibility and such international responsibility must be based on national responsibility. Therefore, the contribution which the independent member states in Africa made to the Congo operation has shown that African solidarity within the framework of the United Nations can build on a strong sense of national responsibility, radiating into the international sphere and creating the interdependence in which independence can yield its most rewarding results.

As to the withdrawal of Belgian troops, Dr. Bunche met on July 19 with the Belgian ambassador in Leopoldville, the Belgian Army Chief of Staff, and the Commanding General of Belgian forces. He told them that in the light of assurances of the arrival of U.N. Forces during the same week in sufficient numbers to protect the entire population, it was necessary that the Belgian forces begin to withdraw completely from the Leopoldville area and return to their bases on July 20. The withdrawal operation was to be completed by 6 p.m. Saturday, July 23.

The arrival of the "International Peace Force" in the Congo was complicated by one important factor as regards its operations. A message of welcome handed to them by Dr. Ralph J. Bunche, Special Representative of Secretary General Dag Hammarskjöld in the Congo, and Major General C. C. von Horn, Supreme Commander of the Force, explained the role of the Force, known as ONUC, derived from the French title, Force de l'Organisation des Nations Unies au Congo. The text of the message said:

> You serve as members of an international force. It is a peace force, not a fighting force. The United Nations has asked you to come here in response to an appeal from the Government of the Republic of the Congo. Your task is to help in restoring order and calm in this country which has been so troubled recently. You are to be friendly to all the people of this country. Protection against acts of violence is to be given to all the people, white and black.
>
> You carry arms, but they are to be used only in self-defense. You are in the Congo to help everyone, to harm no one.
>
> Your conduct should always be such as to do credit to your country and to the United Nations. You are serving the United Nations here. Your orders on this mission will come through your officers only from the United Nations.
>
> You have a great opportunity now to help the Congo and its people. In doing that you will also help Africa. We have confidence that you will do your very best here.[4]

These were hard directions to be given to a soldier, a man used to fighting whenever chaos arises and there is no other obvious way of dealing with the situation. Not even the use of tear gas was allowed in case there was a riot by certain unruly hooligans in the country. This policy probably was the beginning of the constant erosion of the U.N.'s strength; it eventually weakened the organization and invited thereby such an unprecedented deluge of criticism as it had never before experienced in its history. The impartiality of the Secretary General, and what is more, the very office itself, was subjected to doubt and attack. The message, which was printed in English and French, stated that peoples of all races in the Congo, white or black, were to be given protection. This was apparently interpreted to mean that even the rebellious elements in the country were not to be brought back onto the right track, thus laying the ground for uncertainty about legal and illegal authorities in the country. The Secretary General had stated explicitly in the Security Council that the U.N. Force was not to be authorized to action beyond self-defense. It follows further that they were not to take any action which would make them a party to internal conflicts in the Congo.

NOTES: *Chapter 9*

1. Jack Woddis: "Lessons of the Congo," in *Marxism Today*, May 1961, p. 138
2. *Ibid.*, p. 138
3. *United Nations Review*, August 1960, Vol. 7, No. 2, p. 9
4. *Ibid.*, p. 7

CHAPTER **10**

The Widening of the Gap

I OFTEN WONDER whether the world sufficiently appre-
ciates the extent of the revolution which is taking place
in Africa at this time. What seems to me to be unique is
that this revolution is taking place simultaneously on so
many different levels. Political revolution competes with a
revolution in man's environment, that is, in the economic
and social development. The French Revolution was without any doubt a milestone in our human history, but it took
place at a time when men could move about this world
no faster than they could at the dawn of history. The speed
of communication was the speed of the horse or the sailing
ship. Napoleon could move no faster than Hannibal could
two thousand years earlier.

No generation in Africa has been beset with such formidable problems of adjustment as ours of today. This is
why it is so intensely exciting. We have advanced from the
steam engine to the jet plane and the guided rocket at a
bewildering pace. We have reached an age in the advanced
industrialized world where we can bounce messages to
each other off circling satellites with all the obvious advantages that this entails. The same thing has happened regarding sources of power. The same lightning advance has been
made from the telegraph to the television. It is a similar

story in medicine and many other branches of science. Even war, with the coming of nuclear weapons, has been transformed to the point where it can abolish mankind if mankind does not abolish it. Now the age of space exploration is upon us. In view of all this, it is a little hard on the human race when people lament its failure to adjust its social and political institutions to the advances in science, for in all conscience it has been set a most formidable task, and without precedent. All this is of course not yet true of Africa, although the potentialities are there in immense quantities.

In these circumstances, it is not in the least surprising to me that the political and social scene in Africa should be somewhat volcanic. I do not think it is worthwhile for the world to take up much time discussing whether the good old days were really all that good or not. They are gone, and mankind had better adjust itself to living in the revolutionary conditions which are now our lot. Especially must the former white masters of Africa realize the necessity of adjustment. In certain white-dominated areas of Africa, especially the southern part of the continent, the governments are trying to solve the problem of African nationalism through the practice of apartheid, or complete subjugation of the indigenous and dispossessed African majority. For my part, I believe that the totalitarianism of apartheid is a blind alley and will completely fail to provide an acceptable form of society for man to live in. Apartheid is based on the proposition that an African is an advanced type of monkey and nothing more. If we are indeed simply a herd of clever animals, stark materialism should no doubt be our creed. "An African does live by bread alone" is the Afrikaaner—apartheid—claim, and it is a claim that I totally reject. I know of no more striking statement of this fundamental fallacy than that contained in Dostoevski's parable of "The Grand Inquisitor" which appears in *The Brothers Karamazov*. There is made the claim of all totalitarians that mankind's real cry is *"Make us your slaves but feed us."*

The Congo crisis cannot be seen in any other light than this. Western civilization, which apartheid represents and which is now on trial, nevertheless believes that individual man needs far more than physical satisfaction, and nothing that has happened since Belgian colonization of the Congo in1885 causes me to doubt this. The human mind cannot be put in a straitjacket. It will not submit forever to tyranny. A thousand examples demonstrate this truth— perhaps none more strikingly than the Hungarian rising of 1956 when young men and women fought with supreme courage against the Russian tanks, although they had lived the whole of their lives under a totalitarian regime, first Fascist, then Communist. The people of Africa are rising now, and there will be no exception in South Africa or Central Africa. If apartheid is such a desirable system of society, why is it necessary to erect across the country giant barbed-wire fences studded with watchtowers and machinegun posts? Not to keep other Europeans out, so much as to keep the African cherubim in the white man's paradise of apartheid. The truth is that apartheid is not, and cannot be, a panacea for our human ills. One day it will, without doubt, be discarded, but this does not mean that we can afford to be inactive now. The Dark Ages stand as a constant reminder that great civilizations can go down to utter destruction through disunity and inertia, and it is our most solemn duty to see that we leave nothing undone which is needed to insure the survival of democracy in Africa, and the disappearance or transformation of that evil system based on the doctrine of white supremacy and domination.

Debates and events in the Congo in the latter part of July and the whole of August and September, 1960, were such as to cause tremendous pessimism as to the future. The United Nations allowed itself to be completely mesmerized by the cold war. General debates in the Security Council and the General Assembly took definite sides. The late U.N. Secretary General, Dag Hammarskjöld, explained this in his introduction to the annual report on the work of the Organization from June 16, 1960 to June 15, 1961 in document SG/1052. Different concepts of the United Nations, its character, authority and structure, were brought to the fore in the debates by members. The Secretary General wrote that "certain members conceive of the Organization as a static conference machinery for resolving conflicts of interest and ideologies with a view to peaceful coexistence, within the charter, to be served by a secretariat, which is to be regarded not as fully internationalized but as representing within its ranks those very interests and ideologies." Speaking to the other members, who advanced a different outlook, he said that these members "conceive the Organization primarily as a dynamic instrument of Governments through which they should also try to develop forms of executive action, undertaken on behalf of all members, and aiming at forestalling conflicts and resolving them, once they have arisen, by appropriate diplomatic or political means, in a spirit of objectivity and in the implementaton of the principles and purposes of the Charter."

These two concepts produced conflict in the debates. The Belgian delegate, speaking on behalf of Belgium, insisted that the unexpected revolt of the public force had caused a complete deterioration of what had been an orderly situation. He claimed that the force which was the only element capable of maintaining order had been transformed in a very short space of time into an agent of anarchy and insecurity. "It mutinied, and the mutiny spread; the mutineers took over the arms depots and escaped from the control of the responsible Congolese authorities." The most important thing, however, which was going to bring about consequences which were certainly "not happy for my Government, was that certain elements of the public force engaged in odious crime," continued Dr. Walter Loridan. He claimed that people were killed and wounded, women were raped, and other terrible acts committed, such as arbitrary arrests and pillage. The massive exodus of Europeans from the Congo revealed in a startling manner the panic which had gripped them. The European press in Nairobi, as in other parts of the world, was sensational, printing amazingly spectacular stories. The *Sunday Post* in Nairobi of July 17, 1960, printed an article titled "Week of Shame," in which it painted the Congo picture in this way:

> This has been a week of burning, unquenchable shame for all who are concerned with, and who represent, the continuance of civilization in the African continent. Now we know what freedom means. It means freedom to murder, rape and pillage. It means freedom to frighten little children, to tie up old men with ropes and then kick their teeth in. It means freedom to shoot at anything that moves whether it be three or thirty. In a week, Uhuru (which means freedom) has become a dirty word. We class it with Belsen, Hitler and Siberia in the dictionary of distasteful phrases.

Facing the cardinal question as to who is to blame for the

Congo tragedy, and who should be ashamed, the paper continued:

> First, the Congolese themselves for welcoming their independence with an unparallelled reversion to bestiality, for demonstrating that they themselves are capable of nothing more than clawing back the hands of the clock with bloodstained fingers. Second, of course, metropolitan Belgium herself for her weakness and her panic and her indifference to the potential plight of her own kith and kin who were left behind in a bankrupt possession at the moment that the managing director had decided it was no longer profitable. For the Congo, it seems, never meant much more to Belgium than material profit.

In fact I met many white extremist European settlers in Africa who thought that Britain could take almost as much blame as Belgium. They argued that until Mr. Macmillan's wind of change speech in South Africa in 1960 and "the entry of the politically callous and misguided Mr. Macleod into the Colonial Office, Britain was the guiding power in the African destiny. The wind of change can now be seen as the stale imperial flatulence that it is. It was wrong and utterly immoral for Britain to start the 'Uhuru' landslide in Africa and British Parliamentarians can be as smug as they like about the smooth transition to independence in Ghana and Nigeria because the world knows the facts about the Congo. And the facts are murder, rape and plunder while Britain stood indifferently by, and Mac the so called knife, forbade Rhodesian troops to restore order in the Katanga Province when the mayhem reached there." [1]

While these inflammatory reports and speculations went on, chaos continued to dominate the new republic. On July

20-22 the Security Council of the United Nations met again to hear the Secretary General's report, he being the first speaker of that session. The main question was the withdrawal of Belgian troops. The July 14 resolution had demanded Belgian withdrawal but, due to its vagueness, the Secretary General requested a clarification. The Congolese delegate, Mr. Thomas Kanza, in his address to the council, called for the "evacuation as soon as possible—I do not say immediately, but as soon as possible—of Belgian troops from Congolese territory." [2] This position was considered to be a major concession by the Congolese government.

In his opening remarks, the Secretary General noted that the United Nations Operation in the Congo (French acronym: ONUC) was "a most encouraging experience and marks a major step forward in international cooperation, and now we are in a position to look with hope, if not yet with absolute confidence, at the future. We have got off to a most promising start, but we have in no way passed the corner." [3] This optimism was based on the unclear report which arrived at the U.N. Headquarters in New York that Belgian troops had been withdrawn from the major cities where a semblance of order had been restored. It was thought that ONUC, under the general supervision of the Secretary General's Special Representative in the Congo, Dr. Ralph J. Bunche, seemed to be on the way toward the repetition of the success of United Nation's Emergency Force (UNEF). This was later proved to be hardly the case. Not only were Belgian troops not yet withdrawn from any part of the Congo, but there were also signs of foreign unilateral intervention, in addition to that of Belgium, which further complicated the already critical internal situation.

The gravity of the Congo crisis and its importance to the

international community was brought to the realization of
the member nations of the United Nations when Mr. Hammarskjöld made the following statement:

> There should not be any hesitation, because we are
> at a turn of road where our attitude will be of de-
> cisive significance, I believe, not only for the future
> of this Organization but also for the future of Africa.
> And Africa may well in present circumstances mean
> the world. I know these are very strong words, but I
> hope that this Council and the members of this Or-
> ganization know that I do not use strong words un-
> less they are supported by strong convictions.[4]

During the heated debates, the Soviet representative intro-
duced a draft resolution insisting upon the "immediate
cessation of armed intervention against the Republic of the
Congo and the withdrawal from its territory of all troops
of the aggressor within three days," and called upon the
U.N. members to respect the territorial integrity of the
Congo and not to undertake any actions which might
violate that integrity. (Details of the meeting appear in
Press Release SC/2193 and in Doc. S/4402.) Earlier, on
July 14, the Soviet Union had warned of the grave responsibility borne by the leading circles of the Western powers
for unleashing armed aggression in the Congo, and demanded that it should immediately be stopped. The Soviet
note also charged that the North Atlantic Treaty Organization was responsible for "armed intervention" in the Congo
because Belgian troops had been withdrawn from the
NATO defense line in West Germany for duty in the
Congo.[5] All these allegations were, of course, emphatically
and vehemently denied by the Western powers. In the
meantime, more than 2,000 Belgian troops were occupying
Leopoldville and the surrounding Congolese territory.

Twenty-three companies, approximately 3,500 soldiers, were sent to the Congo by Belgium as reinforcements. This constituted, as I have stated above, a clear act of aggression as well as violation of the United Nations Charter.

The Security Council meeting finally adjourned at 1 A.M., July 22, 1960, with the adoption of a mild and watered-down compromise resolution drafted by Tunisia and Ceylon. According to its main provisions, the council unanimously:

> 1. *Called upon* the Government of Belgium to implement speedily the Security Council resolution of July 14, 1960, on the withdrawal of its troops, and authorized the Secretary General to take all action necessary to this effect.
>
> 2. *Requested* all states to refrain from any action which might tend to impede the restoration of law and order and the exercise by the Government of the Congo of its authority and also to refrain from any action which might undermine the territorial integrity and the political independence of the Republic of the Congo.
>
> 3. *Commended* the Secretary General for the prompt action he had taken to carry out the Security Council's first resolution.
>
> 4. *Invited* U.N. agencies to tender to the Secretary General such assistance as he may require.
>
> 5. Requested the Secretary General to report further to the Council as appropriate.

At this time not only intertribal warfare had reached alarming proportions in the Congo, but Congolese troops and Belgian troops were nearly firing on each other. Such a confrontation if allowed to continue could have produced grave consequences for the civilian population. Moreover the Congolese military units, leaderless and without money and food, continued to rampage through the country with all the consequences this entailed. Mr. Hammarskjöld was faced with profound tasks.

The Secretary General had announced on July 19 (Tuesday) that he hoped to leave for the Congo and continue to South Africa on July 23 (Saturday) for talks with the South African government on the question of apartheid which had been condemned earlier by the Security Council as a result of the Sharpeville shootings in March, 1960. Circumstances, however, did not permit this trip, as the Congolese Prime Minister, Patrice Lumumba, had announced in Leopoldville that he was flying to New York for the Security Council meeting. The Secretary General, naturally, had to be available during Lumumba's visit to discuss further development of U.N. assistance to the Congo. Mr. Lumumba arrived in the United States at New York International Airport July 24 at 6:30 A.M. accompanied by Joseph Kasongo, President of the Chamber of Representatives; Joseph Okito,[6] Vice-President of the Senate; and Captain Michel Mawoso, Personal Aide to the Premier.

Apparently, Lumumba made a good impression in the United States despite the accusations in the press that he was a communist. In fact, a settler-controlled paper in Nairobi wrote a fantastic story about him:

> Ask any Belgian refugee why it happened in the Congo and they will give you the answer—Communism. This hated prime minister Lumumba is alleged to be a card carrying Communist. It is reported that in the weeks before independence approximately 1,000 Europeans from Iron Curtain coun-

tries moved into the Congo. They came, it is said, mostly from Czechoslovakia and Yugoslavia . . . as in Communist Guinea. The Belgian refugees firmly believe that they are behind the present trouble.[7]

While these irresponsible stories were being circulated, Lumumba was handling himself with poise and intelligence in the U.S.; he declared to the largest press conference held in the United Nations headquarters that he believed in "positive neutralism." He continued, "We shall accept no assistance from countries which would wish to come to us and set up another regime of domination. We have not come from a colonial regime in order to fall under another dictatorship." [8] Later I came to know the Prime Minister in New York and also in the Congo. He left no doubt in my mind that he was, despite his human mistakes, one of the most passionately dedicated African leaders of his people of whom I know. His ideal was President Kwame Nkrumah of Ghana.

The Secretary General left for the Congo via Belgium on July 28 while the Prime Minister proceeded to Washington to confer with American officials. Mr. Hammarskjöld was not well received in Belgium for two reasons. First, the Congo crisis had had an almost traumatic effect on the Belgian people, resulting in sorrow, indignation, and sometimes frustration. Secondly, the Belgian government was infuriated that Hammarskjöld gave more time to the Congolese Prime Minister—three days in New York—than to the Belgian government—only six hours. This is a small point, but psychologically it was important to them.

Nevertheless, when the Secretary General arrived in the Congo, he found tremendous enthusiasm and support for the Central Government. Banners carrying signs such as "Down with Tshombe," "Quick Liberation for the Congo," and "Total Retreat of Belgians" greeted him on his arrival. When he met with the Cabinet of the Congolese government on July 29, he found tremendous impatience with his slow handling of the Katanga situation and the withdrawal of Belgian troops. In fact it was reported that an open split between Hammarskjöld and the Deputy Prime Minister, Antoine Gizenga, was developing. This prompted the following remarks by the Secretary General on the question of Katanga:

> Do not expect from us actions which might jeopardize the future happiness of those we wish to help. We do not want to assume such a responsibility and we shall not, Ladies and Gentlemen, act in a manner which goes against our convictions, which were based on the thorough study of the problems of the country and its people, and which were guided by the views expressed by their representatives.[9]

The Secretary General repeatedly told the Congolese ministers to "mistrust your feelings of mistrust" and said that in the Congo "one must, generally, mistrust mistrust."

At the end of his visit the Secretary General was optimistic about the situation and said that his conversations in the Congo had been fruitful and encouraging. Although there were difficult points needing reconciliation, they concerned not objectives but methods of evaluation. Among other things, Hammarskjöld said to the Congolese ministers:

> We desire peace in the Congo. We desire calm in the Congo. We desire independence for the Congo, and we offer to the Republic of the Congo all the assistance of which the United Nations and its affiliated agencies are capable.[10]

While the Secretary General was optimistic about a Congo settlement, the Katanga question still remained untouched. This is very important because it was Katanga and Moise Tshombe that caused the widening of the gap between Hammarskjöld and Lumumba. It was in Katanga that Lumumba was brutally and in a cowardly way murdered. It was the question of a Katanga cease-fire which also caused the death of the Secretary General, a very ironical situation indeed! It was Katanga's example which inspired Albert Kalonji to declare the South Kasai "Mining State" independent of the central government. Mr. Tshombe, in his provincial capital of Elizabethville, had not only refused to dismiss the Belgian troops and advisors who were vital to his continued existence, but had announced on August 3 that United Nations troops attempting to enter Katanga would be opposed by force, and said, "they will have to fight their way in." He also called for the mobilization of all able-bodied men in the province to fight against the United Nations troops if they attempted to enter the province. This created a dilemma for the Secretary General. After the failure of the mission on which he had sent Dr. Bunche, to negotiate with Tshombe to allow U.N. troops to land, the Secretary General decided to fly back to New York and ask for specific authorization again from the Security Council. The latter met on August 8-9 to consider the question.

The Security Council heard the Secretary General accuse the Congolese central government of great impatience over Katanga. He recalled that "when I presented to them the reasons why, while acting with the utmost speed, I could not responsibly act more speedily, from many quarters the reaction has been one of distrust, which may well be spread through the population—indeed, there are signs that it has begun to do so—thus creating a most harmful atmosphere. This dangerous tendency of sowing distrust has not been without support from other quarters outside the Congo." [11] The Secretary General requested a clarification of the mandate, and asked whether or not it would cover the province of Katanga, which was only implied in the resolution.

The Soviet delegate not only demanded the use of force against Katanga, but recommended that ONUC should be replaced if it was unable to carry out its instructions. This Soviet statement was probably prompted by the weak interpretation of the previous council resolutions. The Secretary General had given orders that ONUC could only act in self-defense, because he added: "I do not believe personally that we help the Congolese people by actions in which Africans kill Africans or Congolese, Congolese."[12] Although this was well meant and in general the most ethical and ideal thing to do, it was proved later, even before the death of the Secretary General himself, that the bloodshed which he wished to avoid was not, after all, avoided. It would probably have been better to move swiftly against Katanga as Lumumba wanted, and disarm, restrain, and regroup the Congolese National Army, than to have waited through hesitation, wavering, and careful planning under the changing and difficult circumstances. It was further reaffirmed that the entry of United Nations troops into Katanga was necessary for the full implementation of the resolution, but there was another provision that the U.N. force would not be "a party to or in any way intervene in or be used to influence the outcome of any internal conflict, constitutional or otherwise." [13] To me this was completely unnecessary, because later, as we shall see, the United Nations took sides in the dispute. Since the Congo operation was the first of its kind to be handled by the U.N. in Africa, one would be led to believe that the Lumumba government, or probably the man himself, was the guinea pig in this great and dangerous international experiment. The U.N. hesitation and vacillation in the early stages of the operation played directly into the hands of the imperialists. I have never been able to understand why the policies advocated by the late Patrice Lumumba, and which were vigorously rejected by the Organization, are now being pursued in their entirety after his death.

NOTES: *Chapter 10*

1. *Sunday Post*, Nairobi, Kenya, July 17, 1960.
2. UNSC, Verbatim Report on the 877th meeting, Document S/PV. 877, July 20, 1960, pp. 63-65.
3. UNSC, *Ibid.*, pp. 3-5.
4. Press Release SG/935. See also Richard Miller, *Dag Hammarskjöld and Crisis Diplomacy*, The Oceana Library of the U.N., pp. 275-276. Pages 266-315 provide also an excellent summary of the Congo crisis during the critical period.
5. See *New York Times*, July 14, 1960, for article by Seymour Topping, "Russians Demand Troops Quit Congo."
6. Mr. Joseph Okito and Maurice Mpolo were the two men who were later assassinated together with the Congolese Prime Minister in Katanga. A United Nations investigation committee later implicated Moise Tshombe of Katanga and his lieutenants in the murder of Patrice Lumumba.
7. *Sunday Post, op. cit.*
8. *Transcript of Press Conference Held by Premier Patrice Lumumba, Premier of the Republic of the Congo.* United Nations: Office of Public Information, Press Service, July 25, 1960, pp. 9, 14, 17.
9. *Secretary General's Statement at Dinner Given by Vice-Premier of the Republic of Congo.* United Nations: Office of Public Information, Press Services, Sg/937, August 2, 1960, 3 pp.
10. See Press Release CO/20/Add. 2, August 5, 1960.
11. See *New York Times*, August 9, 1960 for Text of Address by Hammarskjöld and Excerpts from Others in Security Council.
12. *New York Times*, August 9, 1960, "U.N. Chief Fears War Over Congo; Opposes Soviet Call for Force; Lumumba Facing Separatist Bids."
13. *New York Times*, August 9, 1960, "Text of U.N. Resolutions on the Congo."

CHAPTER **11**

The Lumumba-
Hammarskjold Split

Moise Tshombe, as we have seen, refused to dismiss the Belgian troops and advisors who were vital to his continued existence and announced that the United Nations troops attempting to enter Katanga would have to fight their way in. Godefroid Munongo, Katanga Minister of the Interior, had also given warning that he would decree full mobilization of the state armed forces should the United Nations defy the warnings from Katanga authorities. In fact, on August 8, Tshombe had rebuffed any attempts by Dr. Ralph Bunche, leader of the Organization's forces in the Congo, to negotiate a peaceful United Nations entry. Their meeting in Elizabethville ended in disagreement, or at least in complete misunderstanding of what had been decided.

Tshombe had conveniently interpreted Dr. Bunche's statement to mean that the Secretary General was to report to the Security Council not only the refusal to allow U.N. troops to enter Katanga, which would have been a sign of surrender on the part of the Organization, but also the case for Katanga's independence. He therefore went ahead and made an announcement which utterly baffled the offi-

169

cials of the World Organization. Tshombe not only demonstrated his own unreliability, but also the fact that he was the tool of imperial interests in Katanga. The U.N., on the other hand, issued a short statement saying that Dr. Bunche had said only that he would report to the Secretary General on the discussions with Tshombe, but he himself could not make any decisions.

It must be assumed therefore that Dr. Bunche had not given any assurances or promises that the Secretary General would report back to the Security Council or that the U.N. troops would not be going into Katanga on Saturday. The decision was Mr. Hammarskjöld's alone and it was unlikely that Dr. Bunche could change his mind by reporting one day's discussions in Elizabethville. There were several things connected with the Katanga affair. Tshombe's opposition to the U.N.'s presence in the form of troops in Katanga—opposition which had been mainly engineered by Brussels—was already well known to Mr. Hammarskjöld before any of his representatives had been sent into the province. In any case, it was clear that Tshombe did not understand fully what was said during the meeting, or else took as definite what was discussed as possibilities only. The *London Times* of August 4, 1960 sarcastically comments that:

> This verbal warfare had been a consistent feature of the Congo situation since it became a crisis after June 30, 1960. Words have been used which have turned out to mean, or have later been said to mean, almost the exact opposite of their customary use. It is a looking glass vocabulary that has made the U.N. task in the Congo much more difficult.

However, let us look into what happened in Katanga

despite all these misunderstandings when Dr. Bunche arrived. The Katanga problem concerns not only the Congo, but also the rest of Africa. To me, and many African nationalists, Katanga is a classic case where a great African stooge or quisling could be turned into an almost complete harp by the colonialists and neo-colonialists: a harp which can be played on at any time, twenty-four hours a day, and will still produce the desired music, no matter how discordant the sound.

On his arrival in Katanga, Dr. Bunche immediately held a meeting with the representatives of the Belgian government in Elizabethville. These included Aspremont-Lynden, the envoy extraordinary, and M. Robert Rothschild, the deputy chief of the diplomatic mission, both of whom had been at the airport to welcome Dr. Bunche. The brief ceremony of welcome at the airport seemed divorced from the harsh realities that faced the U.N. in Katanga.[1] No representative of the provincial government was present, since Tshombe had described Bunche as "an aggressor" whom he would not go out of his way to see. Nevertheless, a detachment of the provincial military police and the army was there. A number of government cars had been sent to drive the U.N. party to their hotel. The new red, green, and white Katanga flag was flown in a number of prominent positions in front of the air terminal. Few people were at the airport except the many representatives of the press and the guard of honor.

To prove Brussels' deep involvement in the secession of Katanga, it should be noted that at the same time that Bunche was holding a talk in Elizabethville, a three-man political delegation was busy lobbying in Brussels for Katanga's recognition and support. The men were Jean-Marie Kibwe, Finance Minister; Joseph Yava, former economics minister of the Congo, and Jacques Masungu, said to be former vice-president of the Senate. They were received by King Baudouin, although it was said they received no indication that Belgium intended to recognize the independence of their state. Mr. Kibwe had visited Paris, where he had been unsuccessful in an attempt to interest the French government in the Katanga independence movement. On his return to Brussels he was received by top government officials, although no promise of Katanga's recognition as a separate state was given. He asserted also that the U.N. would not enter his province, since they had 2,000 well-trained troops which could easily hinder the landing of planes carrying the U.N. troops. "We have very good lions in our forests," he said, "and they would use every means at the disposal of the Katanga government" [2] to stop the establishment of a U.N. presence in Katanga.

During these maneuvers in various Western capitals against the Lumumba government, Belgian diplomats constantly denied having anything to do with Tshombe, a denial which was taken with a pinch of salt by many people throughout the world. For instance, after the Belgian Foreign Minister, M. Wigny, had flown to Paris to confer with M. Couve de Murville, the French Foreign Minister, he returned to Brussels and told reporters that Belgium was "grateful for French solidarity over the Congo," whatever that meant. He was then asked whether Belgian troops would evacuate Katanga if asked to do so. He replied:

> The question of the Katanga is not a Belgian but an African question. We accorded independence to the Congo as an entity. From that moment we have refused any interference in Congolese internal affairs

and we do not have to take up a position on dissentions between Congolese. As for the Belgian troops, they are in the Katanga as in the rest of the Congo to assure security there. The necessity for their presence is therefore a matter within the competence of the U.N.[3]

The extended conflict in Katanga has proved this statement a whitewash. Belgium, as well as Roy Welensky's Federation and other powers, were and have been deeply involved in what has taken place in Katanga. All these events might naturally have angered any prime minister of the Congo, and Lumumba was rightly impatient over these flagrant attempts to dismember his country. The situation became even more worrisome when on August 4, 1960, three conservative British M.P.'s who were known to belong to the former members of the "Suez Rebel Group" requested the recall of parliament after a forty-minute interview with the Foreign Secretary, Lord Home. It was reported in the *London Times* of August 4, 1960, that they wanted parliament to discuss the Katanga situation. Their names were given as Mr. Anthony Fell, Mr. Paul Williams, and Mr. Biggs-Davison. These gentlemen indicated that they wanted the recall of parliament "because of the threat to vital British interests and the peace of Africa arising from the decision to send U.N. troops into Katanga." In a joint statement they said:

> Mr. Tshombe kept order in Katanga. U.N. forces are not needed there, unless they have an ulterior purpose. Why should the peace and resources of Katanga, which has all the qualities of a state, be thrown into the chaos of the Congo—with possibly Communism to follow? Unlike Katanga, Mr. Lumumba's Congo, prematurely recognized, is not a state but

the vassal of U.N. colonialism. We deplore this use
of the U.N. which recalls the tragedy of the Suez.

The intention of many supporters of Tshombe was to
create in the mind of the world the existence of a separate,
harmonious state called Katanga, and to a large extent these
efforts succeeded. The essence of these gentlemen's statement was their dissatisfaction with the position taken by
the British government and they believed that the use of
U.N. troops in Katanga would constitute aggression. This
was undoubtedly an ill-balanced view; the events in Katanga since that time have proved these gentlemen wrong
and Lumumba right. It will be recalled that the U.N. has
been doing just what Lumumba advocated at the very
beginning. It was tragic that the Organization decided not
"to be a party to or in any way intervene in or be used
to influence the outcome of any internal conflict, constitutional or otherwise." [4] This definitely put the U.N. in
a very weak situation insofar as dealing with the law-
breakers was concerned.

The attitude of the Katanga authorities and their support by other Western powers indirectly caused the Secretary General to return to the Security Council in early
August for a clarification of his mandate. The Council's
response was that "the entry of the United Nations forces
into the province of Katanga is necessary" and Belgium
was asked to "withdraw immediately its troops from the
province." [5] On the strength of this resolution and subsequent explanations to Tshombe that ONUC could
neither prevent the national government from subduing
the province by force nor assist in such an endeavor,[6] the
Secretary General himself was able to lead Swedish contingents of ONUC into the province in mid-August. In
the following months this small United Nations presence

which had been established was reinforced by a few additional troops from other European countries. It should be noted here, however, that the U.N. did not succeed in getting the Belgian political advisers eliminated. Moreover, it found itself confronted with Belgian military officers in the provincial armed forces. Later, Katanga began hastily to recruit European mercenaries from all over Europe and Africa to come and fight against the central government. The main recruiting centers were Salisbury, Nairobi, Paris, Johannesburg, and so on. The situation was getting very serious. Tshombe was being armed to the teeth to have his fellow Africans killed by foreign adventurers. This military build-up in Katanga went on, apparently, with the full knowledge of members and officials of the U.N. With this in mind, let us now turn to the relationship between Lumumba and Dag Hammarskjöld.

At this time Lumumba became increasingly impatient with the Secretary General's negotiations with Tshombe, whom he considered a rebel. He, therefore, demanded the dispatch of the U.N. troops to Katanga immediately and proposed a draft resolution under which the Security Council would dispatch to the Congo within twenty-four hours a group of observers representing India, Ceylon, Ghana, Ethiopia, Morocco, Guinea, United Arab Republic, Indonesia, Burma, and Afghanistan. Each country would send one observer and their task would be to insure the strict application of the Council's decisions on the withdrawal of Belgian troops from the whole of the Congolese national territory and more particularly from Katanga.[7] At this point the Secretary General apparently decided to move into Katanga with Swedish contingents only. The Prime Minister complained that he was not even consulted by the U.N. with respect to these latest troop movements, let alone his above-mentioned proposal to the Security Council. The fact that ONUC could not subdue the rebellious province of Katanga also infuriated him, so that by August 15, the ill feeling between the U.N. and the Congolese premier had almost reached a climax. Lumumba bitterly assailed Hammarskjöld and questioned his impartiality about Katanga. He attacked the Secretary General's good faith, charging that "affinities between the Belgian and Swedish royal families" had dictated the use of Swedish troops in Katanga. He then demanded the following things of the U.N.: that all non-African troops should be withdrawn from Katanga; all airports in the Congo be turned over to the Congolese police and army; African troops should be dispatched to Katanga province immediately; United Nations aircraft should be made available to transport national Congolese forces wherever necessary in the interests of peace; and all distribution of arms to partisans of the rebel government in Katanga should be seized at once.[8]

The main dispute between Lumumba and Hammarskjöld arose from the latter's interpretation of a paragraph of the Security Council's resolution of August 9 which reaffirmed in relation to the entry of U.N. troops into Katanga, "that the United Nations force in the Congo will not be a party to or in any way intervene in or be used to influence the outcome of any internal conflict, constitutional or otherwise." The Secretary General's interpretation of the paragraph included these points:

    a. The U.N. force cannot be used on behalf of the central government to subdue or to force the Katanga provincial government to a specific line of action.

    b. U.N. facilities cannot be used to transport civ-

ilian or military representatives, under the authority of the central government, to Katanga
against the decision of the Katanga provincial
government.

c. The U.N. has no duty or right, to protect civilian
or military personnel, representing the central
government, arriving in Katanga, beyond what follows from its general duty to maintain law and
order.

d. On the other side, the U.N. has no right to refuse the central government to take any action
which by its own means, in accordance with the
Purposes and Principles of The Charter, it can
carry through in relation to Katanga.[9]

The Secretary General pointed to the Lebanon and
Hungarian precedents where similar interpretations were
used, to show that in any crisis where "elements of an
external nature and elements of an internal nature have
been mixed," this would be the best interpretation for the
Congo also. The Prime Minister in turn, as I have pointed
out, considered this an "erroneous and unilateral" interpretation of the Security Council resolution to which his government could in no way agree. Instead he demanded
exactly the opposite of what the U.N. Secretary General
had proposed. He considered that through conversations
with Tshombe, the Secretary General had made himself
a party to the conflict and was using the U.N. to influence
its outcome.

The Secretary General sharply rejected Lumumba's demands and said he would not enter into a discussion of
"unfounded and unjustified allegations" in Mr. Lumumba's
letter but would have it circulated as a Security Council
document. Mr. Hammarskjöld was prepared to present his

case in person and hoped the Prime Minister would do
the same should the Security Council wish to take a stand.
The Secretary General explained that the requests which
were submitted by the Prime Minister appeared "to derive
from a position contrary to my interpretations of the resolution." In any case, Mr. Lumumba was strongly of the
opinion that the Secretary General's positions were in no
sense those of the Security Council. He considered that
the Secretary General had decided to inform the central
government of his plans only after making arrangements
with Tshombe and the Belgians, and had refused to give
his government the military assistance for which it had
approached the U.N. The Congolese premier stated later,
on August 15, that "the government and people of the
Congo have lost their confidence in the Secretary General." [10]

Faced with such a profound misunderstanding, the Secretary General had no choice but to return to the Security
Council, which he did. Richard Miller has put the point
succinctly:

> The real issue revolved around whether the U.N.
> force would be a free agent in the Congo or whether
> it would be under the Central Government's direc-
> tion. The Premier was worried that the large build
> up of the U.N. personnel in the Congo would bring
> the country closer to an unofficial U.N. trust terri-
> tory. And in some respects that was happening. He
> objected because it threatened and conflicted with
> his power.

The United Nations Security Council met on August
21-22 to consider the new developments in the Congo. The
intention of the meeting this time was to strengthen the

hand of the Secretary General in the face of trouble with Congolese authorities. The Security Council never took any formal action, but gave Mr. Hammarskjöld the "clarification" he requested, which apparently was also an indication to Lumumba that the Organization was heavily on the side of the Secretary General in the dispute over the question of the role of ONUC in the Congo. At the council meeting, the Secretary General, apparently annoyed by the attacks on his impartiality as an international civil servant, threatened that he would be prepared to recommend the complete withdrawal of ONUC from the Congo if the activities of Mr. Lumumba continued to spread "deep distrust and hostility fomented for political ends."[12] This threat apparently did not serve its intended purpose. Instead, the Congolese Government grew increasingly suspicious of the Secretary General and his representative in the Congo at the time, Dr. Bunche.

I was already in Leopoldville at this time. I had several talks with the Prime Minister and Dr. Ralph Bunche and with other Congolese officials and it became clear to me at once that their views were completely irreconcilable. The question of Katanga was like a great wound, and any talks which did not favor immediate action on Katanga by the U.N. or by the Central Government assisted by the U.N. forces, could not satisfy the Congolese premier. As an African, I fully supported and sympathized with Lumumba's views on Katanga, but I thought that since Tshombe had such efficient support from outside powers, it would be very dangerous for the Central Government to underrate his military strength. Even more, it would be most dangerous for troops of the Central Government to be sent to Katanga without thorough and careful preparation. Several attempts were made to defeat Tshombe militarily, but these failed dismally because of the tremendous build-up he had been allowed to accomplish. In my mind, the greatest mistake, from which the U.N. could not extricate itself, was the refusal to deal with Tshombe's secession at once, since the authority of the legally elected government had been completely accepted by the Organization. But Katanga was treated as a special case, as if it were not a province of the Congolese territory.

When I landed at Bakwanga, in the province of Kasai, accompanied by General Victor Lundula, a great civil war was raging between Albert Kalonji and the Central Government. Several people had been killed, and it was clear from what I was able to observe that the Central Government forces had captured the airport and almost subdued Kalonji's forces. Kalonji himself had escaped in the direction of Katanga. But the problem which posed itself was one of support, in terms of food, equipment, and transport, for the Central Government's troops. Moreover, the few Belgians in Bakwanga were working very effectively in favor of Kalonji, and with the U.N. already confused and having denied its support to Lumumba, the operation was sure to fail. This prolonged the Kalonji problem up to the present time, with constant war going on between the tribes. The world was later that year shocked at the terrible famine in Kasai which killed thousands of women and children, while Kalonji was staying comfortably in a hotel in Brazzaville.

In retrospect, one would be inclined to say that if secessionist movements had been stamped out at once, and the Congolese National Army retrained, the Congo problem would have been an easy one to solve, especially as regards the lack of technical and administrative personnel. Lumumba's demands were, therefore, quite rational; the only problem he faced was his premature disagreement with the U.N. which caused the Organization to work, directly or indirectly, for his downfall.

A very important development in the Congo crisis came when Major General Alexander, a British officer in charge of the Ghanaian contingents in the Congo, issued a note with respect to the role of the U.N. in the Congo. General Alexander, with his experience in Africa, reported to the U.N. authorities in New York that "the immediate and also the long-term possibility of getting the country back to normal hinges on the retraining and disciplining of the Force Publique." He added that "it will certainly be hopeless unless something drastic is done to deal with the Force." [13] General Alexander placed the blame for the situation which had developed on the U.N. commanders who had been quite unprepared to exercise any military authority at all, thus putting Ghanaian and other U.N. troops in an impossible position.

In reply to General Alexander, Dr. Bunche sharply charged that the criticisms, "in the major import, are neither valid nor fair." He also called attention to the fact that the U.N. troops constituted a "peace force, not a fighting force"! Dr. Bunche further argued that General Alexander "takes a fighting man's approach to the U.N. force. It may be that he finds it difficult to comprehend the nature of an international peace force, or of the policy of restraint and cooperation with the Government of the country which must govern the activities of such a force." [14]

History has already proved General Alexander right and Dr. Bunche wrong. The U.N. has fought two battles in Katanga, and the question of disarming and retraining the Force Publique is one of the great interests of the U.N.

at this time. It is the undisciplined elements of the army which violate the whole territory, killing as they pass through. This army has posed and will continue to pose a great problem for the United Nations. It appears, in retrospect, that the views of President Kwame Nkrumah of Ghana, presented to the U.N. in a very eloquent and historic speech to the U.N. on March 7, 1961, would have gone a very long way in solving the Congo crisis had they been fully implemented. The problem is that the cold war has so deeply entered into the Congo crisis that any quick solution would now be very difficult.

The other important achievement of the Security Council meeting of August 21-22 was the suggestion by the Secretary General concerning the establishment of the Congo Conciliation Committee. The advisory committee was to consist of member nations which had contributed manpower to the Congo operation. This committee facilitated a more formal and regular arrangement for consultations, which was very badly needed at this time. The Secretary General also agreed that the geographical distribution in the ONUC was not satisfactory. He explained that this was not due to any discrimination on the part of the organization, but because the people who were needed in the Congo and who were fluent in French could have found the work greatly easier. Nevertheless, he was prepared to accept Communist experts if they were qualified. It was also quite proper that Dr. Bunche should be recalled, as he could now not work harmoniously with the Congolese prime minister. He was replaced by Rajeshwar Dayal, a very capable Indian diplomat.

NOTES: *Chapter 11*

1. *London Times*, August 4, 1960
2. *London Times, Ibid.*

3. *London Times*, August 2, 1960
4. "Text of U.N. Resolutions on the Congo," *New York Times*, August 9, 1960
5. United Nations Soc. S/4426, Aug. 9, 1960. Adopted by 9 votes in favor, none opposed, with 2 abstentions.
6. See United Nations Soc. S/4417/Add. 6, 12 Aug. 1960, para. 8
7. United Nations Soc. S/4422, 12 Aug. 1960
8. Article in the *New York Times*, August 16, 1960, by Thomas F. Brady, "Lumumba Assails U.N. Chief."
9. U.N. Press Release Co/20/Add. 4, 19 August 1960
10. See *Washington Post*, 16 August, 1960, "Hammarskjöld Quits Congo After Rebuffs, Calls Urgent Session," by George Sibera.
11. Miller, Richard I.: *Dag Hammarskjöld and Crisis Diplomacy*. (The Oceana Library of the U.N.: 1961), p. 285.
12. United Nations Security Council, Verbatim Record of the 887th Meeting, Soc. S/PV. 889. August 21-22, 1960, p. 29.
13. U.N. Soc. S/4445, 26 August, 1960
14. U.N. Security Council. Observations by the Special Representative of the Secretary General in the Republic of the Congo on the Memorandum by Major-General H. T. Alexander, Doc. S/4451, August 21, 1960, pp. 2, 3.

CHAPTER 12

Lumumba Is Deposed
and Murdered

DURING SEPTEMBER, 1960, and until February, 1961, when the Prime Minister was reported murdered in Katanga, there followed what many observers called a struggle for power among the Congolese politicians. But in actual fact the breakdown of co-operation between Mr. Kasavubu, the President, and the Prime Minister was engineered mainly from the outside. There was no struggle for power as we understand it in the Western sense of the word. On several occasions I met both the President and the Prime Minister, separately or jointly, and I noticed the greatest desire for co-operation between them for the benefit of the Congolese people. If left alone, Lumumba and Kasavubu could very easily have worked out their differences, as they did just before independence. But we live in a world where the affairs of my neighbor are as much a concern for me as my own. Professor Herbert J. Spiro, writing on this question of the struggle for power between Congolese leaders, said:

> Actually, however, there was very little power for which these politicians could have struggled, even had they wanted to. The Force Publique disintegrated.

The sometime leader of parts of it, Colonel (later General) Joseph D. Mobutu, was treated by representatives of some foreign powers as though he were an up and coming Latin American caudillo or a South East Asian military dictator. He turned out to be neither. His and his sometime partners, sometime antagonists' soldiers were repeatedly reported to be on the verge of mounting a full scale civil war. The war never took place, although there was sporadic intertribal violence of a type that had preceded independence and had never been entirely suppressed by the colonial administration.[1]

On a very bright morning in London on September 5, 1960, I finished my breakfast at the Regent Palace Hotel in Piccadilly Circus, and walked out to buy a newspaper. I had just arrived via Cairo and Paris the previous evening and my mind was still full of Congo politics. Not a moment passed without my thinking about Katanga and what a problem it posed for Africa, and I was still thinking of the eloquent speech by President Kwame Nkrumah to the Ghana National Assembly about the Congo in the middle of the previous month. In fact, when I was in Accra I had the impression that the people there felt more deeply about the Congo crisis and what this meant for Africa, than in any other place. Nevertheless, I nearly wept when I saw in the English newspaper headlines that Lumumba "was out and Ileo in," for it spelled out clearly to me the success of all the maneuvers that had been going on for a long time in Leopoldville to oust the Prime Minister from power. In any case, President Kasavubu had been persuaded to dismiss the Prime Minister, and an acute crisis was sure to follow.

Under the provisions of the *Loi Fundamentale*, The

Chief of State was authorized to dismiss the ministers (Article 22) but the resigning government was required to conduct the affairs of state until its successor was formed (Article 44). It further empowered the Chief of State to adjourn Parliament (Article 31) but only for a period of one month (Article 70). Parliament could not be dissolved without consultation with the Council of Ministers and a two-thirds concurring vote of one of the two houses (Article 71). Questions of the interpretation of the basic law were the "exclusive privilege" of the chambers of Parliament. (Article 51)

Not only were these provisions annulled, but any arguments by those who supported the Lumumba government were met by a deaf ear from the outside world. Instead, the appointment of Mr. Joseph Ileo as the new prime minister was apparently endorsed and approved by the United Nations. Although Lumumba got a vote of confidence from parliament, which also declared the action of Kasavubu null and void, the U.N. argued that the votes were purchased or that there was no quorum. This may or may not have been true. The significant thing is that these same tactics of which Lumumba was accused were also employed by Kasavubu to a greater degree during the crisis.

However, the downfall of the Lumumba government and his final physical liquidation was by no means confined to Congo politics alone. Lumumba had been invariably called a Communist by several Western magazines and newspapers. In fact he became a controversial figure in almost every Western capital and was, I believe, generally dismised as a Communist. That word has a variety of meanings according to the personal views of the man who makes the charge. Some in America (as the John

Birch Society type, for example,) have said that General Eisenhower was a Communist. To others a Communist means simply a person who is in favor of a certain pattern of economic organization in which the state plays a certain active part. Still others mean when they call you a Communist that you are a dedicated agent of what they call an "international conspiracy." Cheddi Jagan, the prime minister of British Guiana, once said to an American audience: [2]

> During your own struggle to get rid of colonialism your leaders were called all sorts of names. For example, if the term had been known in his day, General Lafayette would almost certainly have been called a Communist. Tom Paine, whose writings fired the blood of your revolutionaries and inspired me during my student days here, was charged with seditious libel for publishing the "Rights of Man." An ex-colonial American Chief Justice, John Reeves, set up an organization in England called the Society for the Preservation of Liberty against Republicans and Levellers. And the leaders of your revolution were charged with conspiring with a foreign power—Jacobin France. I draw attention to these aspects of your history because I think it will help you to understand why I have so often been called names and had my views misrepresented and distorted.

Continuing to explain his personal position, Dr. Jagan said: "First of all I am a passionate anti-colonialist. I, like your forefathers, believe that colonialism is wicked. I believe so strongly that colonialism is utterly wrong that I would gladly accept any help from whatever quarter to help me in my fight against it."

As background to this I would say that Mr. Lumumba

was no different. There is no doubt that in 1960 he was the Congolese whose position was most advanced in the direction of "Africanism" and "progressism." He was far from being a fellow traveler but he was undoubtedly the most neutralist among the Congolese leaders. He was very intelligent and possessed an extremely acute political sense, but, lacking all experience of political life, he was basically impatient, and it was this impatience and a certain instability which occasioned his ruin. Mr. Lumumba politically controlled regions of the Congo which, although relatively poor, occupy a central position around the important communications network of Stanleyville. Moreover, he represented the militant and advanced wing of African nationalism and could thus not be left out of any representative and responsible government.

Once a compromise between him and Mr. Kasavubu was found impossible, due to outside interference in the affairs of the Congo, the only alternative for neutralizing such a powerful man was to intern him politically. Dr. Nkrumah, addressing the U.N. on September 23, 1960, had this to say about outside interference in Congolese internal politics.

> I personally and my Government have done everything possible to assist and advise the leaders of the Congo to resolve their differences and place their country's and Africa's interests first. Both of them, President Kasavubu and Prime Minister Lumumba, speak the same language of peace and unity. Both of them are anxious to see stability achieved in their country. Both of them agree to reconciliation. What, then, prevents them from coming together? What has led to the Mobutu episode?

Continuing to answer these questions, the Osagyefo said:

I can assure distinguished delegates that, but for the intrigues of the colonialists, a document of reconciliation which had been drafted in the presence of my Ambassador in Leopoldville and approved by both Mr. Kasavubu and Mr. Lumumba would have been signed by them. Imperialist intrigue, stark and naked, was desperately at work to prevent this being signed. The policy of divide and rule is still being practised energetically by the opponents of African independence and unity.[3]

In any case, several attempts were made to arrest Mr. Lumumba during the period he was under house arrest. Despite the statement issued by the United Nations that the Organization's guard had been granted to the principal political dignitaries of the central government without consideration as to where they stood in the new political crisis or in relation to each other, Mr. Justin Bomboko, the Foreign Minister under the Lumumba, Ileo, and Adoula governments, still threatened that if the U.N. prevented Mr. Lumumba's arrest the Congolese Army would shoulder its responsibilities.

This threat was not only legally sterile, but the U.N. could not change the orders of the guard to facilitate the service of a warrant of arrest which was not *prima facie* valid. The warrant which was issued for the Prime Minister's arrest was definitely invalid because it had been expressly issued against a deputy without prior compliance with the basic law from which the warrant purported to have derived its authority. As a matter of fact, parliamentary approval prior to the arrest of a member of a legislative assembly is normally required in the interest of safeguarding the balance and fabric of the state.

Since these actions were carried out during the military

regime of Major General Mobutu, it can be recalled that when he stepped into the political scene it was emphasized that this action was intended only as a temporary measure to promote a political settlement on a nation-wide basis. It is difficult to reconcile with that aim any attempt to carry out an act of political violence such as the seizure of a prominent political figure without due process of law.

All these clear and consistent violations and complete disregard for the fundamental law of the land caused many Africans outside the Congo to have a very strong suspicion that things were being organized from outside the Congo and had assumed a cold-war character. President Nkrumah summed up the sentiments of many people in Africa when he said:

> It is quite clear that a desperate attempt is being made to create confusion in the Congo, extend the cold war to Africa, and involve Africa in the suicidal quarrels of foreign powers. The United Nations must not allow this to happen. We for our part will not allow this to happen. This is why we are anxious that the U. N., having reached a point where inter-vention on the side of the legitimate Government of the Congo appears to be the obvious and only answer to this crisis, should act boldly through the medium of the independent African States.[4]

President Nkrumah made this suggestion with the hope that the extension of the cold war into the Congo conflict could be avoided if the African States were allowed to act under the canopy of the United Nations. He was con-vinced this could produce very effective results. In fact, he added that it would be negative to believe and hesitate "until the situation becomes irredeemable and develops into another Korea." Dr. Nkrumah even went further and suggested that all financial aid or technical assistance to the Congo Republic should be arranged only with the legitimate government of the Congo Republic, channeled through the United Nations and guaranteed and supervised by a committee of the independent African States appointed by the Security Council who should be accountable to the United Nations.

It became quite clear, after there were indications that none of these recommendations were even considered, that the cold war had deeply divided the United Nations. In the meantime, Prime Minister Lumumba was under arrest in his residence, from which it was later reported that he had escaped in late November, 1960. For about two days the world kept on guessing at what had happened to him. To some it was apparent that he had been murdered, but on December 1 he was reported captured at Port Francqui and brought back to Leopoldville to be transferred to Thysville prison. The Congolese Prime Minister was manhandled, beaten thoroughly, and, to say the least, unspeakably humiliated before the eyes of the world by General Mobutu's troops.

In Thysville prison Lumumba lived under terrible conditions. Conditions which can only be understood when we read his last letter to Mr. Rajeshwar Dayal, Special Representative of the United Nations Secretary General, at Leopoldville. The letter was dated January 4, 1961, and said:

Your Excellency,

I had the pleasure of receiving the visit of a Red Cross doctor on December 27, who intervened energetically on my behalf and that of the other members of parliament who are in prison with me. I duly informed him of the inhuman conditions under which we are living here.

Briefly our position is as follows:—

I am here with seven other members of parliament including the President of the Senate, Mr. Joseph Okito—an official and a chaffeur, ten persons in all. We are held in damp cells which we have not once been permitted to leave since December 2, 1960. The food brought us (twice a day) is very bad and I often eat nothing for three or four days at a time, contenting myself with banana.

I informed the Red Cross doctor whom you sent of this, and moreover, in the presence of a colonel from Thysville, I asked if fruit could be bought for me for my own money since the food is so bad. In spite of the doctor's permission, the military authorities refuse to do so under the pretext that they are obeying orders received from the Chief of Staff, Colonel Mobutu.

The doctor from Thysville prescribed that I take a short walk every evening and thus leave the cell for a short time, but the Colonel and District Commissioner will not allow it. The clothes I have been wearing for thirty-five days have never been washed. I am forbidden to wear shoes.

In a word we are living under wholly unbearable conditions which are also contrary to the law.

Apart from this, I have no news from my wife and do not even know where she is. As decreed by the Congolese Criminal Code, I should receive her visits regularly.

On the other hand, the existing Code of Penal Proceedings applied in the Congo explicitly lays down that the person arrested must be heard by the investigating magistrate within twenty-four hours at the very latest; after the lapse of five days the prisoner must appear once again before the magistrate who will decide whether he will be held in preventive custody or not. After fifteen days the prisoner should appear once more before the magistrate who decides whether to prolong preventive custody or not. The prisoner is accompanied by his lawyer every time.

The law on criminal proceedings decrees that the imprisoned person is "d' office" free if the magistrate fails to bring the decision to prolong preventive custody after the lapse of five days after the arrest is not confirmed after fifteen days.

Since our arrest on December 1, to date we were never brought before an investigating magistrate or judge. No order of arrest was ever shown us. We are held in the garrison prison, where we have been for thirty-four days already, confined in cells formerly reserved for sentenced service-men.

The Law on criminal proceedings has not been respected. The existing legislation pertaining to the treatment of prisoners has not been respected either. This is a purely arbitrary arrest, particularly in view of the parliamentary immunity we are entitled to.

Such is the situation of which I beg you to notify the Secretary-General of the United Nations whom I thank for his intervention on my behalf.

How will it be possible to establish law and order in the Congo if already at the beginning of the RULE OF LAW, human dignity and human life are not respected? Until we are brought before a legally constituted court we remain deprived of the fundamen-

tal right of every citizen to defend his case before
the judiciary institutions of the country.

I remain calm and hope that the United Nations
will help us out of this situation.

I am writing to you illegally on bad paper.

I remain, most respectfully,
Patrice Lumumba, Prime Minister.[5]

In the meantime, the situation in the Congo was deteriorating every hour. The American people had just elected
a new President, and many Africans were still hopeful that
Mr. Kennedy would adopt a much more liberal and realistic attitude toward Lumumba than his predecessor did. But
the Congolese prime minister was murdered before Kennedy took office on January 20, 1961. An army revolt in
Thysville against General Mobutu, supposedly caused by
Lumumba, almost enabled the Prime Minister to get released. He was free for a while around the prison com-
pounds, but never attempted to escape. President Kasavubu
went to Thysville to offer Lumumba a cabinet position
less than premier, but he refused on the grounds that such
an action would be illegal since his government still had
the confidence of parliament. Lumumba still considered
himself the rightful prime minister of the Congolese people.
The result of these upheavals led to a decision by Mobutu
and his supporters to send Lumumba to Katanga on the
argument that it would be safer there than in Thysville.
But in actual case, the Congolese authorities and the United
Nations were completely aware that the Prime Minister
was being sent to his place of torture and death. His arch-
enemy Tshombe, supported by Belgium, controlled Katanga, and many people were almost sure that Lumumba
would be killed on his orders.

On February 13, almost a month after Lumumba and his colleagues had been transferred to Katanga and severely beaten, the world was given very shocking news. Godefroid Munongo, Minister of the Interior in Katanga, announced that the former Premier had been killed by the inhabitants of a village known to be bitterly opposed to his policies. Munongo said that he was killed while attempting to escape, and then added: "The villagers who killed him have rid the Congo and the world of a problem."[6] The Katanga provincial authorities refused to identify the villagers, and instead promised them monetary gifts for having killed Lumumba.

This announcement abruptly ended speculation over the whereabouts of Patrice Lumumba, which had preoccupied the minds of many people for almost a month. One thing was clear, however. The Prime Minister was not murdered by villagers as suggested by Munongo. A report made public on November 14, 1961, by a United Nations Commission that investigated the death of Patrice Lumumba and his two colleagues, had this to say on the role played by Munongo:

> Mr. Munongo, who had been awaiting Mr. Lumumba's arrival, approached him and, after a few remarks, took a bayonet from one of the soldiers and plunged it into Mr. Lumumba's chest. While Mr. Lumumba lay on the ground dying, a certain Captain Ruys, a Belgian mercenary serving in the Katanga army, ended his sufferings by putting a bullet through his head. The witness believed that Captain Ruy's act was purely humanitarian.[7]

The witness further stated that Tshombe had Mr. Lumumba's body taken to a refrigerator at the laboratory of the Union Minière du Haut Katanga, a Belgian mining company. The body was put into a formol. He further stated that it was only some weeks later that the story of the alleged escape and subsequent death of the prisoners was made public. The witness believed that the transfer of Mr. Lumumba and his companions from Thysville to Elizabethville was organized and carried out by a representative of M. Nendeka, Chief of the Sûreté in Leopoldville.

Several witnesses appeared before the U.N. Commission, one of them being a British mercenary who had been captured by the U.N. in Katanga and evacuated from the Congo. He stated that while on leave in Johannesburg from his service in the Katanga gendarmerie, he had learned from his wife that Mr. Russell-Cargill had told her that Mr. Lumumba and his two companions had been killed by the Belgian Colonel Huyghe. When this British mercenary met Colonel Huyghe later, he asked him whether this story was true. Colonel Huyghe admitted, according to the report, that he had shot Mr. Lumumba and his two companions with the assistance of a certain Captain Gat, another Belgian mercenary, and a few other volunteers serving with the Katanga gendarmerie in the area of Elizabethville, in a villa garden, where a few men had gathered for drinks to "celebrate" the arrival of Mr. Lumumba and his companions.

The British mercenary, as reported by the U.N. Commission, added that Mr. Tshombe, Mr. Munongo, and some other ministers were present at the time of the murder, as was Mr. Russell-Cargill. He could not state, however, the exact date of the event, although he supposed it to have occurred on the day the prisoners arrived at Elizabethville on January 17, 1961. He further stated that Colonel Huyghe had told him that the murder had been planned in advance and that the bodies were removed and taken out of town, but no details were disclosed as to the place or means of final disposal.

To prove his point before the Commission, the British mercenary added that Colonel Huyghe had appeared to be very nervous and since then had seen a psychiatrist. And that he carried a loaded pistol at all times and kept hand grenades in his bedroom to resist arrest. The mercenary in question believed Colonel Huyghe's account to be true, and considered it to be corroborated by other indications. For instance, the Commission quotes another British mercenary who confirmed the above reports. He said *inter alia* before the Commission:

> Huyghe then told me the story in the first person. He mentioned that he was present at the execution of Lumumba. I asked him to tell me more, and he carried on by telling me, first of all, that there were Katangese African troops present at the farmhouse where Lumumba and his two henchmen were kept. There was also a Minister present — I cannot remember whether he said Kibwe or Munongo, but I know it was a Minister of importance. He then went on to say that the two lieutenants of Lumumba were brought into a room and were told to pray for their lives, and that they were then shot in the back of the head as they knelt. He then mentioned that Lumumba was brought into the room, and that he himself personally shot Lumumba. He rather stressed the death of Lumumba by stating that when Lumumba walked into the room he started screaming and crying for his life. He turned to everybody in the room and stated that whatever they wanted as a reward he would give them, if he was not killed.

Huyghe's words to me were: "Pray, you bastard!" — excuse the expression, but those were his words to me — "You had no pity on women or children or nuns of your own faith, so pray!" "Lumumba, according to Huyghe, fell on the ground and started rolling and screaming for mercy, and Huyghe said he shot him as he rolled on the ground. I said, "Christ, no, Charley" and he said, "Yes, Roddy, it is so." But I would like to stress here, as I stressed in my report to your legal representative in Leopold-ville, that we had both been drinking and Huyghe at that time might have been bragging — though I would not personally put it past Huyghe to have carried out this act.[8]

The United Nations Commission's report and the witnesses they heard, in spite of their conflicting evidence, seem to fortify the statement I made in an interview with the *Boston Globe* of February 19, 1961. (See Article titled: "Lumumba's Boston Friend—African at Harvard Tells of Talks With Murdered Congo Leader," by Earl Banner.)

After stating that most Africans will view Lumumba's murder as signaling the beginning of a new struggle for release from neo-colonialism, I gave three reasons why I believed that his death was deliberately kept hidden for weeks. These premises were:

1. Just two weeks before Munongo announced the death of Prime Minister Patrice Lumumba, the Katanga government refused to allow the U.N. Conciliation Committee or even the International Red Cross to visit Lumumba in prison although this had been allowed earlier while he was still in Thysville. This refusal could only be justified if the man had already been murdered and Tshombe and his sup-

porters wanted to conceal the matter to the rest of the world.

2. Secondly, the report on his "escape" said he had escaped while being transferred from a prison to a farmhouse. But a later announcement said he had escaped by digging a hole through the mud wall of his prison. These stories were clearly contradictory.

3. Thirdly, nobody knew where Lumumba was buried. There was a growing belief that his body was thrown into the river.

The U.N. Commission's report, which could be said to be impartial, indicates some parallelism with my argument. To clearly understand this, let us see what it said:

> The reluctance of the Leopoldville authorities and those of the province of Katanga to allow the United Nations Conciliation Commission and representatives of the international committee of the Red Cross to visit the prisoners justifies the belief that something serious had happened to Mr. Lumumba and his fellow prisoners and that the Congolese authorities were obviously trying to conceal the truth.

> It is beyond the comprehension of the Commission that President (Joseph) Kasavubu, who had only been just recognized by the United Nations as the legal representative of this country, after strong opposition from some countries, had not intervened effectively to allow the Conciliation Commission and representatives of the International Committee of the Red Cross to visit the prisoners, unless a serious event which was contrary to the generally accepted concept of human rights had already taken place under his authority.

The Commission would also draw attention to the significant fact that the alleged escape of Mr. Lumumba and his two fellow prisoners was made public on the very day on which President Kasavubu had promised to inform the Conciliation Commission of the date on which it would see the prisoners.

In studying the account of the alleged escape of the prisoners, the Commission had the advantage of hearing on this subject, Mr. Knecht, the former senior official of the Katanga government closely associated with Mr. Tshombe.

These reasons given in the above quotation led the Commission, after comparing the evidence given by several witnesses including that of two close members of Mr. (Moise) Tshombe's entourage, not to believe any version of the facts given by the provincial government of Katanga. It should be noted here that the U. N. Commission examined with the greatest attention and impartiality the version of the facts given by the government of Katanga Province.

NOTES: *Chapter 12*

1. Herbert J. Spiro, *Politics in Africa, Prospects South of the Sahara* (Prentice-Hall, Inc., Englewood Cliffs, N. J., 1962), p. 122. An analytical and general treatment of the Congo politics has been discussed in the same book on pp. 115-131. This provides interesting reading for those who wish to hear a different point of view.
2. Cheddi Jagan, "Socialism and Democracy," in the *Monthly Review*, February 1962, pp. 461-466. This was a complete text of an address which Dr. Cheddi Jagan, Premier of British Guiana, delivered to the National Press Club in Washington on October 24, 1961. "In it, Dr. Jagan in effect challenges the United States ruling class to choose between providing aid to an outspokenly socialist regime in an underdeveloped country or exposing its protestations of devotion to democracy as sham and hypocrisy." From the introduction to the article.
3. Text of an address by Osagyefo Dr. Kwame Nkrumah, President of the Republic of Ghana, to the 15th Session of the General Assembly of the United Nations in New York on Sept. 23, 1960. In

supplement with *Ghana Today* of Sept. 28, 1960; (Ghana Gov't. Information Services, London), p. 3. The speech was titled "Africa and World Affairs."

4. Nkrumah's U.N. address, *Ibid*, p. 3.
5. *Labour*, Official Journal of the Trades Union Congress, Hall of Trade Unions, (George Padmore Road, Accra, Ghana, July 1961, Vol. 3, No. 1) p. 7, Lumumba's Last Letter to U.N., Thysville, January 4, 1961. From the Journal: "He was tortured to death, but as brave and gallant African nationalist leader Lumumba was faithful to the Pan-Africanist cause even unto death."
6. Adrian Porter, "Lumumba Massacred in Katanga, *Washington Post*, February 14, 1961.
7. *New York Times*, November 15, 1961, p. 14, "Excerpts From Report by U.N. Commission of Inquiry into Lumumba's death."
8. *New York Times, Ibid.*

Off the Beaten Track?

THE ATTAINMENT of independence by the Republic of the Congo and the ensuing violence brought to the fore a fundamental question. Can newly independent countries adhere to the rule of law or will they revert to arbitrary government? Many people in the Western world argue that many African leaders clamor for freedom, but the only freedom they want is the freedom to impose their will on the people they claim to set free. It is a sad and disturbing fact, the argument continues, that so many of the so-called leaders of these national movements see only one way of achieving their ends—by taking advantage of the inherent liberalism of the European powers to subvert the mind of the great bulk of their people with a coolly calculated campaign of hate, falsehood, and intimidation. An ordered evolution, the argument concludes, which many Africans would appreciate, is not for the extremists because it would deny to many of them the prospects of immediate personal power.

It is true that the fundamental problem of organized society lies in the use and abuse of power. Especially as a country emerges from colonial rule to independence must it consider how best to prevent the abuse of power and direct its use to good ends. By power is usually meant the will and capacity of men to insure the obedience of other men.[1] Power is neither good nor bad in itself, but only according to the ends which it serves. If we follow Dante, then we must believe the great medieval doctrine that the authority of the ruler rests ultimately upon law. But a ruler must nevertheless be armed with power, for law does not extend beyond power. Law without power is a lamp that does not burn.[2]

But did the Congo debacle provide an example of lawless African leaders twisting their newly gotten power for selfish ends? Did the crisis prove that rule by Africans leads to arbitrary government, and that colonial law and order is anyway better than that? No, I don't think so. It cannot be claimed that the Congo's problems were caused by the abuse of power by the Congolese leaders. The problems stemmed from the unwillingness of the colonialists to accept the turn of events in the rest of Africa. After realizing it was too late to resist the independence movement in the Congo, Belgium apparently reverted to neo-colonialist tactics.

The European in Africa has fallen into the terrible habit of thinking that the African does not need his friendship; that he wants to humiliate him; that he desires a parting of the ways. This is not so. In fact it is friendship we crave. Our business is not to throw overboard the slave-holder and tyrant. Our tradition of tolerance in Africa forbids us to do so. Our mission is merely to convert the colonialists. We do not want to break the bond between the colonial powers and Africa, but we do want to transform that bond. We want to transform colonial slavery into complete freedom for our continent.

Nobody in the Congo wanted the dagger of the assassin. Nobody needed the poison bowl, the sword, the spear or the bullet. But the people simply had acquired a will of their own, an ability to say "No" to the Belgian neo-colonialists, and in Patrice Lumumba that nation learned to say "No." Lumumba himself would have meant nothing to the rest of the world if he had not represented a cause. He sought to represent a nation, a great organization of a people that had made itself felt. He was never fired with the spirit of lawlessness, rebellion, or terrorism. On the contrary, it was Lumumba who formed a political organization bereft of any tribal basis. In the Congo nationalism has been aggressive but ethnically parochial. Many of the Congolese political leaders were not anxious for wider and more sweeping political amalgamations, and thus presented a great problem for Lumumba's secular nationalism. In a speech at Stanleyville on August 28, 1960, Lumumba laid down his philosophy of a peaceful settlement of the crisis as far as this was possible. He said *inter alia*:

> I shall hope against hope—I shall strain every nerve to achieve an honourable settlement with Belgium and for my country if I can do so without having to put the millions of my people, women and children, through this ordeal of fire. It can be a matter of no joy and comfort to me to lead you on again to a fight of the character we had in 1959. But I must warn you that if a further ordeal of fire has to be our lot again in order to ward off Belgian aggression, then I shall approach that with the greatest joy and with the greatest consolation that I was doing what I felt to be right, and the country will have the additional satisfaction of knowing that it was not . . . taking lives, it was giving lives; it was not making the Belgian people directly suffer, it was suffering.[3]

It is clear, therefore, that the Congolese people and their

leaders had no desire to engage in violence. Instead of capitalizing on the crisis and saying, with a frown, that the Congo is off the beaten track, the world should realize that the Congo is a fundamental case representing many of the problems faced by the rest of the African countries, although in these countries the problems have not been brought out as dramatically as in the Congo.

I do not pretend to have read history, but as a schoolboy, I had to pass a paper in history also, and I read that the pages of history are soiled red with the blood of those who fought for freedom. I do not know an instance in which a nation came into its own without having to go through an incredible travail. The dagger of the assassin, the poison bowl, the bullet of the rifleman, the spear, all the weapons of destruction have been used by what I consider blind lovers of liberty and freedom, and the historian has not condemned such lovers. The Mouvement National Congolais—Lumumba's party—came upon the scene following the tactics of civil disobedience as proclaimed in the Accra Conference of 1958. But Lumumba came up against a stone wall and was told that his was a method no government in the world would tolerate. To give further illustration of the stone wall erected by European colonists in Africa, let us examine what Sir Roy Welensky, the Federal Prime Minister, said recently of African nationalism:

> Pan-Africanism will not rest content until what they call European domination is swept from the whole continent. It is one of the most blatant exercises in racialism the world has ever seen and has brought nothing but evil in its train. It is power that the Pan-Africanists want, never mind the price. A man's race is to count, not his ability. The evil inspiration of Hitler is forgotten, his theories of racial super-

iority . . . and the tragedy is that this new form of
racialism is respectable in the eyes of the world
simply because those whom it serves have succeeded
in giving it the name of freedom.[4]

Sir Roy continued by saying that because the Pan-
Africanists used the name of freedom the Western powers
had failed to see the conflict in Africa as part of the struggle between East and West and that because the lesson
of appeasement in the 1930's had been forgotten, and above
all because there had been "a slip from morality and courage in world affairs," the architects of disorder had had
their way in Africa. Sir Roy opposes those men in the
Western world whose answer to Africa's problems is what
he calls abject surrender—surrender of ethics, standards,
and everything the British way of life stands for. He takes
the position that the effort to make the Western world
aware of the "sorry history" of recent times and of the
dangers of today must be continued and redoubled (sic).
In his view, there can be no compromise in the struggle,
for compromise would mean defeat.

While there is yet a little sand left in the glass, I want
to suggest in all humility that it is utterly impossible for
such extremists of European descent in Africa to find a
meeting ground with African nationalism. The two cannot
find a ground where they can apply the spirit of compromise.

It is true that the problem of our generation is the elimin-
ation of race as a significant factor in the evaluation of men.
The eighteenth century was a battle for political freedom
and laissez-faire individualism; the nineteenth emphasized
economic equality and opportunity; while the twentieth
represents a struggle for racial equality. Because racial

discrimination has restricted both economic equality and personal liberty, the struggle for racial equality inevitably involves the other two. In this respect African nationalism has a wider significance and moral dimension which is fundamental in our age, and which brings political freedom in Africa very close to the social problems which engulf great countries like America. The European colonialists in Africa, with their hankering after symmetry and logical tidiness to justify their oppressive regimes, often distort the truth in order to mislead the world. Very simply, all Africa desires is freedom—political freedom and racial dignity and stature. These are the only means by which the hunger to be free of social discrimination and invidious slurs on culture, history, and the African personality can be satisfied. That the African right to independence has been widely recognized was clearly stated in Prime Minister Macmillan's "Wind of Change" speech in South Africa early in 1960. He said:

> What is now on trial is our way of life. Our judgment of right and wrong and of justice is rested in the same soil as yours—in Christianity and in the rule of law as the basis of a free society. It has been our aim to create a society which respects the rights of individuals—a society in which men are given an opportunity to grow to their full stature, and that must in our view include the opportunity of an increasing share in political power and responsibility; a society finally in which individual merit, and individual merit alone, is the criterion for a man's advancement, whether political or economic.[5]

The above is illustrative of the problems which the Congo, like other African states has to face. It is granted that there are some very special problems in the Congo that are not faced by other countries in Africa. I am thinking specifically of the lack of well-trained administrative personnel and political leaders. It is not without significance that under the colonial administration, and the system of education in the Congo was one of the vital features of paternalism, African illiteracy was not substantially reduced. In fact, the course was firmly set against anything that might encourage the emergence of what are sometimes called "black Europeans." This was definitely responsible for the immediate breakdown of the Congolese administration after independence. However, the more important point to stress is that even if well-trained administrative personnel had been available in the Congo, her fundamental problems would still not have been solved for the colonial powers would still have accentuated the tribal differences and played on the emotions attendant to such diversity in the country.

First and foremost was this danger of tribalism. Many Africans and their leaders have realized the virtues of secular nationalism as opposed to traditional and ethnically parochial tribal-nationalism. The problems of the Congo throw much light on the phenomenon of secular nationalism, and it is natural to ask if it is possible to fuse relevant groups of different color, tribe, and culture into one stable society. This has been the basic question of community or nationhood. Now, if we assume that it is possible for the various groups to live together peacefully in one community, can that community be organized on a democratic basis? These are questions which African countries, like all other countries in the rest of the world, must try to solve if the basic problem of community is to be answered adequately. In his appeal for national unity against tribalism after the assumption of power as the Prime Minister of the present Ghana, which was broadcast to the nation on June 23, 1954, Dr. Kwame Nkrumah said:

> To progress one of the necessary ingredients is coop-
> eration, and I ask you all, of whatever tribe, race,
> colour, creed or political party, to work together
> for the future of the Gold Coast.

This warning was well timed. No African can fail to appreciate the dangers of tribalism. In the Congo, except for one leader, the late Patrice Lumumba, all politicians have tended to obtain their support from one tribe only. Mr. Lumumba was the only leader with a national outlook.

Secondly came the issue between constitutionalism and arbitrary government in the Congo. The rapid and open flouting of the *Loi Fundamentale* by secessionist activities in the Congo presented the spectacle of the rule of law being replaced by arbitrary and physical compulsion which was at the ruler's disposal. Without law the people are ruled by fear. This point is worth laboring because to me the most fundamental issue in Africa today is not whether we shall have a capitalistic system or a socialistic one, but whether we shall be ruled by law at all, or only by arbitrary will. Problems posed by power led historians like McIlwain to write:

> Never before in its long history has the principle of
> constitutionalism been so questioned as it is being
> questioned today, never has the attack upon it been so
> determined or so threatening as it is now. The world
> is trembling between the ordinary procedure of law
> and the processes of force which seem so much more
> quick and effective. Never in recorded history, I be-
> lieve, has the individual been in greater danger from
> government than now.[6]

Because of the problem of power many historians have suggested two methods of taming power which they believe to be particularly relevant to the problems now bedeviling Africa. First, they propose the entrenchment and judicial enforcement of a Bill of Rights in a rigid constitution, and secondly, federalism as opposed to centralism. A Bill of Rights is a method which depends for its success on putting effective legal checks upon power, whereas federalism, though also placing legal restraints upon power, goes further by dividing it, seeking to tame it by balancing one part against another.[7]

I do not believe that we can rely solely on the efficacy of constitutions in Africa because there are cases in the world where these have primarily remained on paper without being applied. Let us take the example of industrialization. In any attempts by any nation to industrialize, it must be remembered that the lesson which economists have learned the hard way through economic history is that no nation can simply import the industrial revolution from abroad, uncrate it like a piece of machinery and set it in motion. Some of the skills, the equipment and the money may come from external sources. External pressure may impose the necessity to remake traditional economies; foreign example may stimulate the ambition to raise productive power and economic well-being. But the real motive power of change must come from leadership and creative enterprise emerging from within. The outside world can only supply the missing component.

Similarly, by adopting a constitution patterned after the Belgian one, without due consideration of local conditions, the Congo found herself in tremendously deep water. Moreover, it is manifestly foolish, and I would add politically illiterate, to place too much confidence in the efficacy of constitutions. No constitution can artificially fuse racial groups into one healthy community, one nation or shared society, if in fact the operative currents are flowing too strongly in a different direction. No constitutional reforms in any colonial country are likely to be of much more than academic significance unless they first grapple with far more basic problems, i.e. consider the plain facts of existing power under European domination, and of winning the good will and genuine co-operation of the African people. This is very important because of the inevitability of the triumph of majority rule; otherwise, constitutional reforms could be nothing more than an attempt to create unity between a cat and a dog by tying their tails together in a constitutional knot.

Nevertheless, it must be realized that secessionist movements in the Congo and their support were derived from two other sources apart from the above constitutional incompatibilities. First is the case where a province has economic advantages of natural resources which she does not want to share with the rest of the country. In this way such a province can retain, hopefully, such wealth by seceding from the rest of the country (as in the case of Katanga Province). Secondly, is the case where power politics or political rivalry based on personal ambition and hunger for power between the national leaders dominates the interests of the nation. This type of situation plays directly into the hands of the neo-colonialists. Neither of these motives deserve praise.

In Africa we have made clear our desire to steer a middle course between the East-West contest. Pan-Africanism offers to us an ideological alternative to Communism on the one hand and tribalism on the other. It would be politically and economically foolish for the African continent to remain divided, thus perpetuating the political boundaries which were drawn by the colonial powers when they were dividing the continent among themselves. These boundaries were drawn regardless of the natural and ethnic similarities. In the post-independence era, these boundaries will have to be redrawn to account for ethnic unity. Any tendency to revert back to small communities, acting independently of each other, will greatly retard economic and political progress. I therefore would urge a new politically integrated African community to replace outdated national selfishness. Must we wait for another great catastrophe, greater than the Congo debacle, to produce the necessary compression of our sovereignties, the critical mass from which great new political energies should emerge?

The division between the so-called Monrovia and Casablanca powers is unnecessary because it serves only the purposes of those who would like to drive a wedge between African states. It encourages too much of the canceling effect of national cross-purposes. It is high time we seek between inertia and utopia a practical common course to harness our several national strengths in the cause of peace. Under the present practice, African leaders meet at relatively long intervals, usually in an atmosphere of semi-crisis and then go back to their national preoccupations. Private citizens pour out rhetorical statements; new committees are established, but the key problem remains—national selfishness doubting that such a positive political act of faith is needed and the postponement of the necessary self-denial until sometime in the future. I believe strongly that until the African nations put behind them the illusion that purely consultative relations are adequate in this nuclear era, real political progress will be hard to come by.

In retrospect, one would conclude that the Congo crisis demonstrated quite vividly the bankruptcy of the Belgian colonial policy for over eighty years. Colonialism in any shape or form always means robbery, exploitation, and flouting of the elementary rights of the people and their national sovereignty. Colonialism means ignorance and hunger. I have always believed that the only solution to the problem of African advancement is the adoption of a truly democratic system in which merit is the sole criterion. The Congo crisis clearly indicated the unfortunate fact that the attention of the world is usually focused on peoples or countries only when their problems reach the stage of tragedy or explosion. And it is a very sad commentary on human nature that dramatic and tragic developments mean little more than headlines in the world's press. At the moment, little is being said or done about the terribly repressive measures in Mozambique by the Portuguese or in South Africa where a powerful Afrikaan-speaking section of the dominating white group whose Calvinistic religious and political thought, with their uncompromisingly anti-equalitarian character, has carried out consistently and on a limited scale the act of genocide. Although genocide dates back to the sacking of Carthage or even earlier, this crime of crimes "has represented itself with the regularity of a biological law." But it was left to our own generation to see it practiced on its largest scale by Hitler. It is known that Dr. Verwoerd, the Prime Minister of South Africa, sympathized with Hitler's racial policies. I remember when I was in London on November, 1960, after leaving the Congo for the United States, a friend with whom we were discussing the Congo situation remarked angrily:

> The policy of the Belgian government in the Congo crisis is undoubtedly a policy of aggression and pil-

lage. It can only be compared with the behavior of a bandit who is strong and can do anything he wants with his victim. I hope that you Africans will not for long be unable to uphold your dignity. I am sure you will soon have everything necessary to render any aggressor harmless if only you are united.

NOTES: *Chapter 13*

1. B. de Jouvenel, *Power*, (London, 1952). See Chapter 1 dealing with the metaphysics of power.
2. See the quotation by Sayers in her introduction to the Penguin edition of the *Divine Comedy*, Hell, p. 45, in *De Monarchia.* See also *Law as a Means to An End*, Husik's translation.
3. The speech was made in Swahili and I was among the audience then. So far as I know, it was never reported in any Western press. Lumumba also condemned violence against Europeans on this occasion because the day coincided with the beatings by Congolese troops of five Americans and one Canadian who had landed at Stanleyville airport. The troops thought that they were Belgian para-commandos.
4. See *London Times*, February 3, 1962, p. 8, the article on "Uncompromising Mood Over Surrender in Africa."
5. *Souvenir of A Visit.* Printed on the authority of Mr. Speaker, Cape Town, see pp. 8-11. A reply by Dr. Verwoerd, the South African Minister, is also published in this pamphlet. This is an extremely important document because it shows the divergence of views between the two men with respect to African advancement. It is hardly necessary to say that Sir Roy Welensky's attitude is not very far removed from Dr. Verwoerd's.
6. MacIver, *Constitutionalism, Ancient and Modern*, 1947, p. 1. Quoted also I. V. Cowen, *The Foundations of Freedom, Law and Government in Southern Africa.* Professor Cowen's book presents the best analysis of the problems of law and government with specific reference to Africa that I have read in a long time.
7. I. V. Cowen, *Ibid.*, p. 85.

CHAPTER **14**

What Next?

THE INTEREST that is now being shown in the international position of Africa is in itself proof of the presence of a new force on the world stage. Obviously Africa did not appear by magic, nor is it given itself momentarily to a more or less felicitous exhibition of publicity seeking. When I refer to "a new force" I am not alluding to a military one, but to the fact that a continent, heretofore almost unknown, is prepared through positive neutrality to bring to bear, on the play of world pressures, the economic and human potential it represents and the knowledge reaped from experience that we have a right to believe is of positive value.

Africa is a nation of continental proportions, occupying an area four times the size of the United States of America, and only second to Asia in size. The Congo, being just a small part of it, occupies an area almost the size of western Europe. Within the coming decades, the biological revolution by which population has begun to grow in an unprecedented way will herald a new era, and the rapid industrialization of some regions—what Barbara Ward calls the application of capital and science to all the processes of earning man's daily bread—will herald our development into an economic power. At present we are still beset by the evils of underdevelopment which made the greater part of our continent the scene of great political dramas. We have poverty-stricken areas which are overpopulated, we have vast regions—the largest in the world—still unexplored or unconquered. And yet our great cities are becoming industrial and trade centers of major significance.

The Congo crisis was a clear manifestation of the revolution of equality that obtains all over Africa. One of the most remarkable facts about our time is that colonialism, as a recognized principle of political domination, is on its way out. This, I believe, will be the greatest peaceful political revolution that mankind has ever seen. It has been said that since conquest has been man's oldest and most endemic activity, if we can rid ourselves of it, we shall have done away with nine-tenths of the causes of war. The complete liquidation of colonialism would, therefore, contribute immensely toward the achievement of international peace and security. As Albert Luthuli once said, ours is a continent in revolution against oppression. And peace and revolution make uneasy bedfellows.

There can be no peace in the world until the forces of oppression are overthrown. Our continent has been carved up by the great powers, and this has created a situation in which there can be neither peace nor the brotherhood of men. As long as the laws of certain nations virtually criticize God for having created men of color, there can be no peace. Now, the revolutionary stirrings of our continent are setting the past aside. Our people everywhere from north to south, from east to west of the continent, are reclaiming their land, their right to participate in government, their dignity as men, their nationhood. Thus, in the turmoil of revolution, the basis for peace and brotherhood in Africa is being restored by the resurrection of national sovereignty and independence, of equality and the dignity of man.

This is why the West and the East must support us unconditionally in this peaceful revolution of ours. It should not be difficult for the West to appreciate this, since their own revolution stretched across all the years from the eighteenth century to our own, encompassing some of the bloodiest civil wars in all history. Comparing the European revolution and the Congo crisis, for example, the latter appears relatively peaceful and mild. The African revolution has swept across three quarters of the continent in less than a decade, and its final completion is within sight of our own generation. Again, by comparison with Europe, our African revolution to our credit is proving to be orderly, quick, and comparatively bloodless.

Nevertheless, the Congo crisis has deeply awakened the African people to the great dangers of neo-colonialism. In view of the revolt that obtains all over Africa, nothing allows us to believe that the imperialist powers are going to discontinue their economic, political, and military enterprises. The belief created in the minds of many of our people as a result of Belgian unilateral intervention in the Congo is that Africa occupies a preponderant place in the expansionist plans of the imperialist powers. By subtle maneuvers and sometimes under the guise of economic agreements, these powers appear to be pooling their resources and co-ordinating their efforts for the building of military bases in our countries. These things are indispensable for the exploitation of the immense resources they foresee. President Sekou Toure of Guinea summed up at the U.N. General Assembly on October 10, 1950, the sentiments of many Africans when he said:

Thus, colonialism tends to take an international shape that tolerates flags and hymns of African nationalism and anthems, but will not allow one finger to be placed on its own interests. Political independence in itself does not mean complete national liberation. Certainly it is a decisive and necessary step forward. However, we must recognize the fact that national independence presupposes not only political liberation but, over and above all, total economic freedom. No social progress is possible without these two conditions. In order that Africa can become economically free, it has not longer to be considered as a reservoir of raw materials. We must underscore the present state of under-development in the quasi-totality of the African continent, with a direct consequence of the absence of a typically all-African economy.

This clearly indicates the deep feeling Africans have about colonialism. As long as a single foot of African soil remains under foreign domination, I suppose the world shall know no peace. We can safely assume that no system of political frustration in Africa will last more than ten years. We have seen the Congo example, where for eighty years Belgium applied a system of political castration in the hope that it would be completely impossible for African nationalists to fight for emancipation. The same thing is happening in South Africa, Angola, Mozambique, and Southern Rhodesia. But to the dismay of Belgium, and to the surprise of everyone outside the African continent, this dreaded nationalism appeared and within a lightning space of time, secured the independence of the Congo.

Since the beginning of the Congo disaster, the balance of forces within the Congo, itself, Africa, and the United Nations has changed substantially. We are now faced with a new situation. A new Congolese government of national reconciliation has been formed under the leadership of Cyrille Adoula. Mr. Adoula is said to represent the forces of moderation inside Congolese politics, so that many westerners look at the future with some ray of optimism. Mr. Antoine Gizenga is temporarily out of the political scene, although still within striking distance of the prime ministership, unless, as it were, his present internment becomes a physical one. Let us hope it will only be political. Tshombe and Kalonji are still very dangerous wounds in the Congolese picture, and one is not always sure what the following day has in store for the U.N. in Katanga. The American government, under the enlightened and liberal leadership of President John F. Kennedy, has adopted a policy more favorable toward Africa than its predecessors. With all these considerations in mind, the picture is still, nevertheless, very confused, so that a speculation on what would happen next must await a second volume of this book. One thing is certain, however, and that is the fall of the so-called President Tshombe of Katanga. There will be no peace in the Congo until Tshombe and those who support him outside the Congo are brought to see what is good for Africa and its peoples.

Mr. Adoula has very wisely built the framework of his foreign policy on the foundations laid down by Mr. Lumumba: that is, positive neutralism. It has been charged by most westerners that positive neutralism is one of those rather rotund phrases which does not readily admit definition. They argue that if, when we say that a nation is neutral, we mean that it will not under any circumstances take arms in any conflict which does not concern the protection of its immediate boundaries, it seems to be a nation hard to reconcile with the Charter of the U.N., which contemplates under certain circumstances the use of combined force in terms of the Charter itself.

This, however, is not what we mean by the phrase positive neutralism. Many governments subscribing to this policy maintain large defenses in their own countries and are active supporters of the Charter. What we actually mean, and have constantly and consistently made clear, is that we stand for nonalignment, in the sense that we will not engage in any special military or quasi-military alliance. But on the other hand, I would think it impossible to believe that any human being can be neutral in the great conflict of ideas or ideologies, since we are influenced by them in the universities and colleges, in the corridors of international associations, and conferences, wherever we come into contact with peoples of diverse make-ups.

Nevertheless, positive neutralism in the political or military sense is the only good thing for the Congo, or for Africa. We must give up the subsidiary and innocuous diplomacy of nations aligned with worthy though alien interests and, to protect our rights, place ourselves in the forefront, convinced as we were before colonization of our ability to contribute with our own means to the understanding of peoples. Africa had been relegated unjustifiably by the colonial powers to an obscure position and now we must reassert our dignity and the African personality. For us to be genuine in this, our foreign policy as such must be the embodiment of the ideals and common interests that govern our existence. Idealistic aspirations are defined by the explicit or implicit establishment of the goals aimed at. They reflect the common interests and the economic, social, historic, and political circumstances that at a given moment influence the choice of immediate aims and the selection of ways and means of action. In Africa, still in a state of underdevelopment, we must not indulge in dreamy consolations while struggling against mighty odds to achieve the full possession of our wealth and develop the potentialities of our own nature. While in the arena of international politics, we must be alert, aware, and vigilant. We must not lose sight of our objectives, yet must avoid jeopardizing them by submitting to policies which, though in keeping with remote ideals, do not at the moment, satisfy our true interests.

We have no right to dream. Rather it is our duty to work—but at the same time to trust and hope—and work with our feet firmly on the ground. Otherwise I cannot see real independence in Africa anywhere on the horizon.

Addendum

Since I finished writing the first volume of my *Lumumba's Congo*, certain events in Katanga—including the change in the United Nations' attitude—have completely corroborated my basic contentions. Until recently it was frequently said that those who criticized the United Nations for its actions in Katanga seemed to have forgotten the original circumstances in which the World Organization was asked to intervene in the Congo situation. It was further said that such critics failed to take into account the conditions under which for a long time the U.N. Secretary General had to conduct the Congo operation.

But the success of U Thant's mopping-up operation in Katanga and the apparent swift collapse at last of Tshombe's secession have come just in time to provide incontrovertible evidence that my demand for the use of force "in the last resort" to bring about the reunification of the Congo was a valid approach. The publication of Dr. C. C. O'Brien's *To Katanga and Back* also supports my basic contentions. The previous failure of the U.N. to apply paragraphs A.1 and A.2 of the resolution adopted by the Security Council on February 21, 1961 effectively, seems to lend further evidence to the fact that those who were previously responsible for carrying out these policies were using, as it were, the paradox of equivocation in the service of virtue. Dr. O'Brien describes these people colorfully as the "Machiavellis of peace; the disinterested Talleyrands."

Nevertheless, there is also evidence which connects the end of Katanga's secession with the emergence of the New Frontier in America's capital. The political acumen of President Kennedy and his army of intellectual-politico-advisers infused new blood into the international scene. As de Tocqueville said, Americans are fortunate in that they arrived at a state of democracy without having to endure a serious democratic revolution, and that they have always been born free without ever having to become so. In other words, due to the absence of forces (like feudalism) which make for economic and social retrogression, as well as the lack of any past social revolution in their lives, Americans are said to have no sense of the role of catastrophe in social change.

Consequently, their approach to such things as the Congo crisis was gradualist—they believed, as it were, in settling the Congo crisis gradually by debate and reason. But the emergence of the New Frontier infused a new element into American foreign policy which drastically changed the whole Congo operation. It was adequately realized by most informed people in America that the Congo question had developed into a classic example of the sort of inter-national situation which leads to world conflict: hence the unequivocal support which the new Democratic Adminis-tration gave to the U.N. and the U Thant plan in the face of some very strong British opposition and equivocation.

But there were also some exceptions. Senator Thomas Dodd of Connecticut was one of the strongest critics of the U.N. military operation in the Congo. He called it "a direct intervention in the internal affairs of a member nation." As reported in the *Manchester Guardian* of Janu-ary 1, 1963, he maintained the U.N. was deporting Euro-pean civilians from the Congo without due process of law, *habeas corpus*, right of appeal, or means of redress, and thus introduced an appalling precedent in the name of the organization dedicated to the rule of law in international affairs. Senator Dodd was also reported to have repeated the more controversial charges that the U.N. forces massacred Christian missionaries in Kongolo in January, 1962; that the U.N. helped to transport the Crizenga forces that seized Albertville in November, 1961; that they also prevented the expulsion of the Ghanaian Embassy when it was supposed to have been helping "the machinations of Lumumba"; that the Baluba refugee camp was set up by U.N. representatives "as a club over President Tshombe's head"; and that the U.N. forces were guilty of atrocities in the September and December, 1961 fighting.

The attitude of Senator Dodd towards African nationalism in general and the solution of the Katanga question in particular is mentioned merely to indicate the fact that he might have been a powerful nuisance to the New Frontier Administration in Washington. This, simply for two reasons. First, because he is probably the only American Senator who is so well informed about the Congo and secondly because, being a Yankee Democrat, his motives are never in question. He has been the chief opponent in Congress of the American Congo policy, and it is even said that he was ready to call a sit-down strike in Congress against funds for the Congo in particular and for foreign aid in general.

But to those who have been intimately connected with the Congo operation these charges could be considered old stuff, and to the U.N. they are mostly repetitious nonsense. However, in the American Congress they can be inflammable stuff, and Senator Dodd was, and still may be, determined to ignite them. There was much suspicion and criticism of Mr. Kennedy's December military mission to the Congo, but it was defused and weakened by the scattering of the old Congress to the grass roots.

In any case, the swift collapse of South Katanga and its major towns has indicated, if anything, that Mr. Tshombe, though personally a charming fellow who had developed almost an "aristocratic" nose, is basically a weak and incapable stooge who was built up into something he could never be by the Union Minière's publicity machine. In fact, he would have long ago vanished into thin air by his natural weightlessness if Britain and other Western European countries had not tethered his expensive propaganda with a legal and constitutional weight he never deserved. Again, the neo-colonialists backed the wrong horse in Africa under the wistful impression that it was a fine public-school type. There is no doubt that the colonialist and imperialist lion in Africa has become a wolf which will soon change into a cat and vanish into the Sahara Desert.

Those who have argued that the use of force in Katanga by the U.N. to subdue Tshombe is a clear demonstration that the World Organization may soon be let loose like a wolf on other nations can hardly claim that this is a sane prognostication of U.N. activities in the world. In fact it was to counter such a result that the Security Council invited the U.N. Secretariat to cope with the Congo problem which it was unable to handle itself and which was threatening to erupt into a major international conflict. Unless action was taken, there was the possibility that the internal tribal squabbles could have revived the spectre of an international confrontation between the Great Powers. If, therefore, I appeared to have scathingly criticized the early phases of U.N. operation in the Congo, it was simply because I wanted to see some vigorous action taken against

Tshombe in order to reunify Katanga with the rest of
the Congo. If Katanga succeeded completely in its secessionist demands, and at the encouragement and the instiga-
tion of reactionaries everywhere, then it would have been
a complete demonstration of a master plan of the neo-
colonialists and imperialists to dismember the new countries
of Africa. Although the political activities of the U.N. in
the early stages in the Congo is still subject to very serious
analysis and criticism, there is no doubt in anybody's mind
that at all times during which the U.N. was involved in
the Congo, it rendered great humanitarian and social services in such areas as famine relief, technical rehabilitation,
administration, education, etc. The only danger lay in the
lack of recognition in the Secretariat of some elements of
human vanity. Too much power was concentrated in the
hands of a few foreigners who had no knowledge of Africa.
Their only image of Africa was one of a people who is in-
eradicably backward and superstitious; a people not very
far removed from barbarism and savagery. As a result of
this, it can be said that many U.N. employees in the Congo
thought of the Congo as a rather dreadful place in which
they had to work for ends of transcendental importance;
the safeguarding of world peace and the survival of the
U.N. itself. (See O'Brien, *op. cit.*, p. 71.) Writing about
the late Dag Hammarskjöld's conception of his office and
himself, O'Brien says in pages 66-67:

> By the very high, and at the same time strangely
> empty, concept of his role which he had propounded
> at Oxford, he was demanding of himself to be both
> more and less than a human being, to be a kind of
> supranational angel. So high and unreal a concept, so
> tense and exigent a conscience, must have made the
> realities of flesh and blood and history—and the mak-

ing of practical political calculations which could not afford to be always so very lofty—something of a torture.

W. A. Okumu
King's College,
Cambridge University,
England
January, 1963.

APPENDIX A

The Speech of Premier Lumumba on Independence Day

LADIES AND GENTLEMEN OF THE CONGO who have fought for the independence won today, I salute you, in the name of the Congolese government.

To all of you, my friends who have struggled continuously on our side, I ask you to make this day, June 30, 1960, an illustrious date which you will keep indelibly engraved in your hearts—a date of which you will proudly teach your children the significance so that they in their turn may make known to their sons and grandsons the glorious history of our struggle for freedom.

Because this independence of the Congo, as it is proclaimed today in agreement with Belgium—the friendly country with whom we stand on equal terms—no Congolese worthy of the name will ever forget that independence has been won by struggle, an everyday struggle, an intense and idealistic struggle, a struggle in which we spared neither our forces, our privations, our suffering, nor our blood.

This struggle of tears, fire, and blood makes us profoundly proud because it was a noble and just struggle, an indispensable struggle to put an end to the humiliating bondage imposed on us by force.

Our lot was eighty years of colonial rule; our wounds are still too fresh and painful to be driven from our memory.

We have known tiring labor exacted in exchange for salary which did not allow us to satisfy our hunger, to clothe and lodge ourselves decently or to raise our children like loved beings.

We have known ironies, insults, blows which we had to endure morning, noon, and night because we were "Negroes." Who will forget that to a Negro the familiar verb forms were used, not indeed as with a friend, but because the honorable formal verb forms were reserved for the whites?

We have known that our lands were despoiled in the name of supposedly legal texts which recognized only the law of the stronger.

We have known the atrocious sufferings of those banished for political opinion or religious beliefs; exiled in their own countries, their end was truly worse than death itself.

We have known that there were magnificent houses for the whites in the cities and tumble-down straw huts for the Negroes, that a Negro was not admitted in movie houses or restaurants or stores labeled "European," that a Negro traveled in the hulls of river boats at the feet of the white in his first-class cabin.

Who will forget, finally, the fusillades where so many of our brothers perished or the prisons where all those were brutally flung who no longer wished to submit to the regime of a law of oppression and exploitation which the colonists had made a tool of their domination?

All that, my brothers, we have profoundly suffered.

But for all of that, we who by the votes of your elected

representatives have been approved to direct our beloved country, we who have suffered the colonial oppression in body and heart, we say to you, all of that is henceforth finished.

The Congo Republic has been proclaimed and our beloved country is now in the hands of its own children.

Together, my brothers, we are going to begin a new struggle, a sublime struggle which is going to lead our country to peace, prosperity, and grandeur.

Together we are going to establish social justice and assure that everyone receives just remuneration for his work.

We are going to show the world what the black man can do when he works in freedom, and we are going to make the Congo the center of radiance for the whole of Africa.

We are going to awaken to what the lands of our beloved country provide her children.

We are going to re-examine all the former laws and from them make new laws which will be noble and just.

We are going to put an end to the oppression of free thought so that all citizens may enjoy fully the fundamental liberties provided for in the declaration of the Rights of Man.

We are going to suppress effectually all discrimination, whatever it may be, and give to each person the just place which his human dignity, his work and his devotion to his country merit him.

We are not going to let a peace of guns and bayonets prevail, but rather a peace of courage and good will.

And for all that, beloved compatriots, rest assured that we will be able to count not only on our enormous forces and our immense riches but also on the assistance of many foreign countries with whom we will accept collaboration so long as it is honest and does not seek to impose any politics whatever.

In this domain, even Belgium who after all understands the meaning of history has not tried to oppose our independence further and is ready to give us her help and her friendship; and a treaty with this understanding has been signed between our two equal and independent countries. This co-operation, I am sure, will be profitable to both countries. While remaining vigilant, we will be able for our part to respect the promises freely given.

Thus, as much at home as abroad, the new Congo which my government is going to create will be a rich, free, and prosperous country. But in order that we may arrive at this goal without delay, I ask all of you, legislators and Congolese citizens, to assist me with all your strength.

— I ask all of you to forget the hazardous tribal quarrels which exhaust our strength and make us contemptible to the foreigner.

— I ask the parliamentary minority to help my government with a constructive opposition, and to stay strictly in legal and democratic channels.

— I ask you finally to respect unconditionally the life and well-being of your fellow citizens and of the foreigners settled in your country; if the conduct of these foreigners leaves something to be desired, our courts of justice will be prompt to expel them from the territory of the Republic; if on the other hand their conduct is good, they must be left in peace, because they also work for the prosperity of our country.

The independence of the Congo marks a decisive step toward the liberation of the entire African continent.

There, Lord, Excellencies, Ladies, Gentlemen, my

brothers in struggle, my compatriots, there is what I have wanted to tell you in the name of the government on this magnificent day of our complete and sovereign Independence.

Our government, strong, national, popular, will be the hope of this country.

I invite all Congolese citizens, men, women, and children, to devote themselves resolutely to their work with a view toward creating a national economy and building our economic independence.

Homage to the Champions of National Liberty!

Long live African Independence and Unity!

Long live the Independent and Sovereign Congo!

APPENDIX B

The *Conscience Africaine* Manifesto

The editorial staff of *Conscience Africaine* has devoted many of its meetings to studying the difficult problems of the future of the Congo.

We are only a small group, but we think we can speak in the name of many because we have voluntarily limited ourselves to delivering and giving form to the aspirations and sentiments of the majority of thinking Congolese.

We have done this in a spirit of sincerity and with a desire to produce a constructive piece of work. What is more, we do not lay claim to any monopoly either of the love of our country or of clairvoyance for her future.

The present manifesto is only a point of departure. We will sharpen and complete it together with those who come later to join us.

Our National Vocation

In the history of the Congo, the last eighty years have been more important than the millenniums which have preceded them. The next thirty years will be decisive for our future. It would be vain to base our national sentiment on attachment to the past. It is toward the future that we turn our attention.

We believe that the Congo is called upon to become a great nation in the center of the African continent.

Our national vocation: to work in the heart of Africa to establish a new, prosperous, and happy society on the foundations of an ancient clan society which has been vigorously shaken by too rapid an evolution, and which now seeks its new equilibrium.

We will only find this new equilibrium in the synthesis of our African character and temperament with the fundamental riches of Western civilization.

Only the Congolese, with the brotherly assistance of the Western people living in the Congo, can realize this synthesis.

In order to speak of a Congolese nation composed of Africans and Europeans, it is necessary that all be filled with the desire to serve the Congo. We have a right to demand of those Europeans who share in our national life to be, above all, Congolese citizens—that is to say, not to pursue only the good of the Belgian community and their own personal interests in the Congo, but to seek, together with us, the good of the great Congolese community.

Unity in Diversity

One principle is essential for us: the color of the skin confers no privilege. Without this principle, union is impossible.

But a fundamental equality does not signify identity: we wish to be civilized Congolese, not "dark-skinned Europeans." We understand well that the Europeans wish to maintain their own way of life.

To uphold the privileges for one of the two groups would be a source of conflict. Not to recognize their individual characters, but rather to want uniformity in them, would create equally dangerous tensions. It must be admitted in a spirit of understanding that a difference does not necessarily imply inferiority or superiority.

We reject with vehemence the principle of "equal but separate"! It is deeply offensive to us. The European and African milieus must recognize the precise nature of one another. Human relations based on equality must be established—not only at the level of the individual, not only in the associations especially created to maintain these relations, but equally in all family, professional, and social contacts.

A Noble Task to Pursue

Out of Belgium's civilizing actions in the Congo will develop a new civilization which will be ours. Already the principal elements of Western civilization are penetrating the Congo more and more intensely. Elementary education is reaching the masses, while an intellectual elite pursues its university study. The unceasing progress of science and technology struggles against illness and misery and establishes the foundations for a growing prosperity. The Christian religion teaches us the profound meaning of life, the eminent dignity of the human being, and the brotherhood of all men.

But we are still only halfway—we want a complete civilization. An increasing number of Congolese want to take more responsibility and more initiative on the future of their country. They wish to assimilate in their national life other basic values of Western civilization which are still absent or insufficiently developed: respect for the individual and for his fundamental liberties without racial distinction; a more intense pursuit of social justice; a true

democracy based on the equality of all men, and the participation of the people in the government of their country.

This is a long-term program which can be accomplished
through the union of Africans and Europeans living in the
Congo.

Belgo-Congolese Community?

We state as fact that Congolese public opinion reacts
with a certain distrust when one speaks of a "Belgo-Congolese Community." These words can cover very different
realities.

To put it more clearly, the Congolese who reflect on
these problems fear that some people distort the idea of
the Belgo-Congolese community in order to put a brake
on the total emancipation of the Congolese people.

For us the vision evoked by Governor General Petillon
is only an ideal of which we dream for the Congolese
nation of tomorrow: A human fraternity based on the
fundamental equality of men without racial distinction.

Progressive But Total Emancipation

Belgium must not consider that there is a feeling of
hostility in our desire for emancipation. Quite to the contrary, Belgium should be proud that, unlike nearly all
colonized people, our desire is expressed without hatred
or resentment. This alone is undeniable proof that the work
of the Belgians in this country is not a failure.

If Belgium succeeds in leading the Congo to total emancipation intelligently and peacefully, it will be the first
example in history of a colonial venture ending in complete
success.

But to achieve that, the Belgians must realize now that

their domination of the Congo will not go on forever. We protest strongly against the opinion sometimes expressed in the press that does not make an essential distinction between the *presence* of the Belgians in the Congo and *their domination* of the Congo.

To those who ask: How long before the Belgians must leave the Congo?, we answer: Why do certain Belgians pose the question to either dominate or abandon completely?

To those who pose this question, we would like to propose for the good both of the Congo and of the Belgians in the Congo, that they pack their bags without further delay.

It is time that the European elite react vigorously here in the Congo, and perhaps still more in Belgium, against such a dangerous mentality.

Whose fault is it if already too many Congolese are sure that the Europeans will not be able to abandon their attitude of political domination, economic exploitation, and racial superiority?

Political Emancipation

We have read that there is a question of a thirty-year plan for the political emancipation of the Congo. Without declaring ourselves on the whole of its component parts, we believe that such a plan has become a necessity if it is the intention to realize emancipation in peace and concord.

This plan should express the sincere will of Belgium to lead the Congo to its complete political emancipation in a period of thirty years.

Only an unequivocal declaration on this point will preserve the confidence of the Congolese toward Belgium.

This plan, which would be a compromise between the

impatience of one group and the conservatism on the other, must clearly establish the intermediate stages which it will effect in fixed periods of time. It is the only way to avoid having each reform project give way periodically to discussions, bargaining, and tests of force between two antagonistic blocs, which, finally, would become irreconcilable.

As for political emancipation, we think that there is a way to depart from the existing institutions by having them evolve progressively. The direction is twofold. On the one hand, existing institutions must become more and more representative by replacing progressively the present system of nominations with a system in which the population itself will designate its representatives. On the other hand, the councils which are now purely consultative must receive a true power of decision and control in increasingly extended matters in order to arrive finally at a responsible government at the head of our nation.

Not giving genuine responsibilities to the representatives of the people would only multiply the difficulties and prepare the future poorly. Those who never sought to undertake decisions on their own have always tended to assert exaggerated and unrealizable claims. This would lead inevitably to demogogy.

We are not asking only for a plan of political emancipation, but for a full plan of total emancipation.

At each stage of political emancipation there must be a corresponding stage of economic and social emancipation, as well as progress in education and culture. The parallel realization of these steps is an absolute necessity if political emancipation is to be sincere and effective.

We do not wish that external appearances of political independence be in reality only a way of enslaving and exploiting us.

Economic and Social Emancipation

Who would dare to speak of real emancipation if the direction of all economic life, the ownership of industrial, agricultural, and commercial enterprises, were to remain indefinitely and exclusively in the hands of the Europeans?

We will not accept the maintenance of a policy of low salaries which permits companies to reinvest a large part of their enormous profits. It would be equally inadmissible to confiscate a part of the just salary of the workers for the profit of a state-socialist economy.

Some people extol "nationalization" of the large enterprises. We have no confidence in this capitalism of the State. Besides, are the workers in Europe much better paid and treated in the nationalized enterprises than in the private firms?

Salaries and agricultural revenues must increase in such a way as to allow continually augmented savings. The Congolese themselves will thus also have a way to raise capital by degrees, to have profits from it and to share in its influence.

Congolese artisans, merchants, and farmers must be encouraged and aided. The middle classes are an important element in the economic and social life of the Congo. For the mass of the population which remains in the villages, consideration must be given to the agricultural economy, and village life must be made more agreeable—beginning by suppressing the loathsome system of forced cultivation.

For the mass of workers, the minimum legal salary which does not permit a decent life must be rapidly raised, especially in the cities where living is expensive. These minimum salaries must be based not on the budget of an unmarried person, but on that of a family. It must be so even for the unmarried adults in order that they may collect the money necessary for marriage without having to deprive themselves to the extent of going hungry.

The possibilities for formation and improvement must be considerably amplified not only by professional education at all levels, but also by a better organization of apprenticeships in the companies.

Beyond the essential minimum, the salaries must bear a realistic relation to the qualifications and efficiency of the worker. For those who meet the qualifications of the Europeans, the chasm which separates the two schedules of remunerations must be bridged.

The Congolese family, which has so much difficulty in liberating itself from the servitudes of the past, is subjected to such conditions of existence in the cities that a bright outlook is impossible. In the domain of housing, particularly, the State has made great efforts, but the problem remains very serious and we have numerous grievances concerning the adopted solutions.

In the past, paternalism has been a necessary thing. The Congolese are beginning to be conscious of the social responsibilities which they can and must take upon themselves. We ask not only that this tendency, which marks a favorable social evolution, not be thwarted, but also that the free organizations which the Congolese have created by their own initiative may be encouraged. We ask, in particular, for the freedom to unionize.

Our Attitude With Regard to Belgium

We are grateful to Belgium, but an artificial patriotism is not asked of us.

To the question of whether we wish to remain united with Belgium later, we answer: "We do not wish in any

way to have the Congo integrated into the united Belgian
state. We will never allow a Belgo-Congolese Federation
to be imposed on us without our free consent, or as a
condition of our political emancipation."

We wish that one day such a community might be the
fruit of a free collaboration between two independent
Nations which are bound by an enduring friendship.

We do not measure this friendship of Belgium by mounting capital investments, but by the attitude of the Belgians
in the Congo with regard to the Congolese, and by the
sincerity with which Belgium will help us to realize our
total political autonomy.

A year ago the Congo reserved a triumphal welcome
for King Baudouin. All the Congolese understood that our
King loved his people. Our cheering expressed not only
our gratitude, but also our hope that the attitudes of the
Sovereign would serve as an example to all Belgians in
the Congo and in the mother country.

Order and Respect for Authority

It is our intention that the Congo's emancipation will
be realized in order and tranquility. And we believe that it
is possible.

We have decided not to let ourselves be drawn into
violence, because violence produces insoluble problems.
We have only one aim: the good of the Congolese nation.
We will make this aim triumphant in lawfulness and by
peaceful means. Those who use violence show that they
are not ripe for true democracy.

We wish to continue to respect authority, but we want
our opinion to be asked more than in the past; we want
it given consideration, and if it is deemed impossible to
follow us, we want to be told why.

We ask specially to be directly concerned, in the most formal way, in the elaboration of the contemplated thirty-year plan. Without this participation, such a plan could not have our assent.

Appeal to the Europeans

Europeans must fully understand that our legitimate desire for emancipation is not directed against them. Our national movement is not inspired by hatred but by brotherhood and justice.

We know that the realization of our hopes will depend on our own efforts, and we will not fail to remind the Congolese often of the harsh truth that we are able to demand our rights only if we are fully conscious of our duties and our responsibilities.

But the Congolese community of tomorrow, composed of whites and Negroes, is realizable only in an environment of respect and mutual esteem, as well as sincere friendship.

To achieve this, many Europeans must modify their attitude toward the Congolese. We believe that this is possible. Moreover, we are pleased to acknowledge that there have been some obvious improvements in the last few years; but they are the doing of too small a number to create wholly the environment necessary for a sound community.

We ask the Europeans to abandon their attitude of contempt and racial segregation, to avoid the continual annoyances of which we are the object. We ask them also to abandon their attitude of condescension which wounds our self-respect. We do not like being treated always like children. Understand that we are different from you and, although assimilating the values of your civilization, we still wish to remain ourselves. We ask from you also an effort to understand our legitimate aspirations and to help us in realizing them.

"The hand offered too late risks being refused," proclaimed Governor General Jungers in a solemn warning. We believe that for a sincere joining between Europeans and Congolese, it is not too late, but it is time.

We note with satisfaction that an increasing number of Europeans are inclined to concede progressively to the Congolese all the responsibilities that they show themselves capable of assuming. Many Europeans also, inspired with a sincere spirit of justice, are willing to share the wealth more abundantly with the Congolese as their more qualified and more productive work helps to augment it. Unfortunately these Europeans are too often left powerless because of their compatriots' lack of understanding.

As a willing group of Congolese and Europeans, by our constructive efforts we will convince those who remain indifferent to our community's future. As for those who persist in an attitude of egoism and contemptuous pride, we will constrain them if necessary by the just and worthy use of the invincible force of our united front.

Need for the National Union

We have only one chance to make our cause triumphant: that is to be and to remain united.

United we will be strong, divided we will be weak; it is the future of the nation which is at stake.

National union is necessary because the whole population of the Congo must, before all else, be conscious of its national character and its unity. How will this be possible if the people are wooed by several competing parties?

This leads us to take a position concerning the introduction of Belgium's political parties into the Congo. Our position is clear: These parties are an evil and they are useless.

Political parties do not fulfill any need in the present political and administrative structure of the Congo, since we have neither a Parliament nor elections. Furthermore, the Belgian political divisions do not have significance for the Congo; they have arisen from historical circumstances peculiar to Belgium.

But above all we do not want parties at present because what characterizes parties in conflict, while what we want is union.

If we let ourselves be divided, we will never realize the ideal of a great Congolese nation. Even if certain parties include political emancipation in their program, the mere existence of these parties is a radical obstacle to this emancipation.

Those Congolese who would be tempted to let themselves get drawn into party politics do not realize the old adage adopted by all dominators: "Divide and conquer"—To divide in order to dominate better.

Let our position be understood: We wish to be neither "a party against parties" nor "an unrivaled party."

We are convinced that it is wholly possible for pagans, Catholics, Protestants, Salvationists, Mohammedans to agree on a program of common good which respects those principles of the natural ethic engraved on the soul of every man worthy of the name. The Congolese can realize this program most surely by being united and by having sincere respect for the convictions of each person.

Later, when the political structures of the Congo make it necessary we can group ourselves according to our affinities, our interests, and our political conceptions. It is highly probable that when that time arrives the specifically Congolese parties will not take the Belgian parties as a model.

How to Realize This Total Union?

To begin, we hope that the present manifesto will stir up among the Congolese, and also among the Europeans, a vast movement of opinion which will crystallize around our modest newspaper. We have already decided to enlarge our editorial staff so that it may be more representative of all opinions compatible with the principles here summarized.

Nevertheless, we are convinced that in the more or less near future, it will be necessary to give a more precise form to the advancement of the ideas we wish to promote, and that there will have to be an organization. This organization will be able to form sections, affiliate members, and hold meetings, in order to realize the considerable work of education which is indispensable in the service of the elite and the masses of our people.

The organization which we anticipate would come into being in full legality, conforming to the laws and regulations in force.

While waiting, we invite our readers, Africans and Europeans, to write to us in order to begin the colloquy. We would be especially happy to learn their point of view on the opportunity for the *Mouvement National Populaire* which we propose.

May those who share our ideal, even if they do not share all our positions, subscribe immediately to *Conscience Africaine* and become propagandists of our journal.

Appeal to the Congolese

Our appeal is addressed first to the large elite which already exists in the Congo and which we believe truly capable of being the leaven among the masses.

We count on those who have had the privilege of studying and who are in teaching, office work, and administration. We count especially on our Congolese university students who are studying in the universities of the Congo and Belgium.

But we want also the miners, the timber-yard workers, the factory workers, the farmers, the artisans, and the merchants. Among them also there rises a true elite absolutely necessary to the country.

May no one among us seek, in the movement we are endeavoring to create, his own interests or the satisfaction of his own ambitions.

We must accept, generously, and distinterestedly, to be at the service of our people. That is not an abstract and vague reality; there is a vast group of men, women, young people, infants who live around us, whom we must love profoundly and whom we must help with all our power to rise and advance.

We must not be satisfied with words. It is not sufficient to write and shout in order to realize our ideal. Extended efforts, sown with difficulties and thwarted by disappointments, will be necessary. Tenacity, perseverance, and patience will be equally necessary.

Through our dignified, intelligent and courageous attitude, through our respect for authority and for the men who represent it, we wish to merit esteem and confidence in order that all will rally to the cause we wish to promote.

We have full confidence in the future of our country.

We have confidence also in the men who must live in it in concord and in happiness.

With all the sincerity and all the enthusiasm of our hearts we cry out: Long live the Congo! Long live Belgium! Long live the King!

About The Author

W. A. Jalango Okumu was born in a missionary hospital in Maseno, Kenya, twenty-six years ago. His father was a health inspector before becoming a prosperous merchant and a prominent local politician. Washington Okumu is one of seven children. He attended a missionary high school twenty miles from his home where he passed the Overseas Cambridge School Certificate in 1956.

About his schooling in Kenya, he writes: "At this time I already had a reputation for proficiency in the English language, the only handicap being a flair for grandiloquent words and complicated phraseologies. I was quite shy and not much given to speech except for occasional curious anecdotes. But my English teachers thought that I could make a successful career in journalism because of my facility with the language. On finishing I worked with the Ministry of Works in Kenya and was elected by African workers to be a Joint-Staff Chairman in the same Ministry to represent them on labor and housing problems. This made me aware of the appalling poverty and backwardness with which my people had to contend. I thought I could serve them better by receiving higher education, so I began to study for Higher Cambridge by correspondence after working hours and at the same time making plans to go to America for higher studies."

In 1958 Mr. Okumu went to Wesleyan College in Iowa where he made the Dean's List every semester and was named the most prominent freshman at the end of the academic year. In 1959 he won a scholarship to Harvard University where he graduated *cum laude* in Economics in June, 1962. He is now a Commonwealth Scholar at King's College, Cambridge University. Mr. Okumu has traveled widely, including the Caribbean and Latin America and he has served under Kenya's Jomo Kenyatta as an Executive Officer in the Ministry of Economic Planning.